FIFTH EDITION

GRAMMAR *in* CONTEXT

SANDRA N. ELBAUM

The cover photo shows the
San Francisco-Oakland Bay
Bridge over San Francisco Bay
in California.

HEINLE
CENGAGE Learning™

Australia • Brazil • Japan • Korea • Mexico • Singapore • Spain • United Kingdom • United States

HEINLE
CENGAGE Learning

Grammar in Context 2B, Fifth Edition
Student Book
Sandra N. Elbaum

Publisher: Sherrise Roehr

Acquisitions Editor: Tom Jefferies

Development Editor: Sarah Sandoski

Technology Development Manager:
   Debie Mirtle

Director of Global Marketing: Ian Martin

Director of US Marketing: Jim McDonough

Product Marketing Manager: Katie Kelley

Marketing Manager: Caitlin Driscoll

Content Project Manager: Andrea Bobotas

Senior Print Buyer: Susan Spencer

Project Manager: Chrystie Hopkins

Production Services: Nesbitt Graphics, Inc.

Interior Design and Cover Design:
   Muse Group, Inc.

© 2010 Sandra N. Elbaum

Library of Congress Control Number: 2009936998

ISBN 13: 978-1-4240-8091-5

ISBN 10: 1-4240-8091-6

Heinle
20 Channel Center Street
Boston, Massachusetts 02210
USA

Cengage Learning is a leading provider of customized learning solutions with office locations around the globe, including Singapore, the United Kingdom, Australia, Mexico, Brazil, and Japan. Locate our local office at international.cengage.com/region

Cengage Learning products are represented in Canada by Nelson Education, Ltd.

Visit Heinle online at **elt.heinle.com**
Visit our corporate website at **www.cengage.com**

Printed in the United States of America.
1 2 3 4 5 6 7 8 9 10 — 13 12 11 10 09

Contents

Lesson 3

Lesson 4

Lesson 5

Lesson 6

Lesson 7

Lesson 8

Lesson 9

Lesson 10

Lesson 11

Lesson 12

Lesson 13

Lesson 14

Appendices

Index

Acknowledgments

Many thanks to Dennis Hogan, Sherrise Roehr, and Tom Jefferies from Heinle Cengage for their ongoing support of the *Grammar in Context* series. I would especially like to thank my development editor, Sarah Sandoski, for her patience, sensitivity, keen eye to detail, and invaluable suggestions.

And many thanks to my students at Truman College, who have increased my understanding of my own language and taught me to see life from another point of view. By sharing their observations, questions, and life stories, they have enriched my life enormously.

This new edition is dedicated to the millions of displaced people in the world. The U.S. is the new home to many refugees, who survived unspeakable hardships in Burundi, Rwanda, Sudan, Burma, Bhutan, and other countries. Their resiliency in starting a new life and learning a new language is a tribute to the human spirit.—*Sandra N. Elbaum*

Heinle would like to thank the following people for their contributions:

Elizabeth A. Adler-Coleman
Sunrise Mountain High
  School
Las Vegas, NV

Dorothy Avondstondt
Miami Dade College
Miami, FL

Judith A. G. Benka
Normandale Community
  College
Bloomington, MN

Carol Brutza
Gateway Community
  College
New Haven, CT

Lyn Buchheit
Community College of
  Philadelphia
Philadelphia, PA

Charlotte M. Calobrisi
Northern Virginia
  Community College
Annandale, VA

Gabriela Cambiasso
Harold Washington College
Chicago, IL

Jeanette Clement
Duquesne University
Pittsburgh, PA

Allis Cole
Shoreline Community
  College
Shoreline, WA

Fanshen DiGiovanni
Glendale Community
  College
Glendale, CA

Antoinette B. d'Oronzio
Hillsborough Community
  College-Dale Mabry
  Campus
Tampa, FL

Rhonda J. Farley
Cosumnes River College
Sacramento, CA

Jennifer Farnell
University of Connecticut
  American Language
  Program
Stamford, CT

Gail Fernandez
Bergen Community College
Paramus, NJ

Irasema Fernandez
Miami Dade College
Miami, FL

Abigail-Marie Fiattarone
Mesa Community College
Mesa, AZ

John Gamber
American River College
Sacramento, CA

Marcia Gethin-Jones
University of Connecticut
  American Language
  Program
Storrs, CT

Kimlee Buttacavoli Grant
The Leona Group, LLC
Phoenix, AZ

Shelly Hedstrom
Palm Beach Community
  College
Lake Worth, FL

Linda Holden
College of Lake County
Grayslake, IL

Sandra Kawamura
Sacramento City College
Sacramento, CA

Bill Keniston
Normandale Community
  College
Bloomington, MN

Michael Larsen
American River College
Sacramento, CA

Bea C. Lawn
Gavilan College
Gilroy, CA

Rob Lee
Pasadena City College
Pasadena, CA

Oranit Limmaneeprasert
American River College
Sacramento, CA

Linda Louie
Highline Community
  College
Des Moines, WA

Melanie A. Majeski
Naugatuck Valley
  Community College
Waterbury, CT

Maria Marin
De Anza College
Cupertino, CA

Michael I. Massey
Hillsborough Community
  College-Ybor City Campus
Tampa, FL

Marlo McClurg-Mackinnon
Cosumnes River College
Sacramento, CA

Michelle Naumann
Elgin Community College
Elgin, IL

Debbie Ockey
Fresno, CA

Lesa Perry
University of Nebraska at
  Omaha
Omaha, NE

Herbert Pierson
St. John's University
New York City, NY

Dina Poggi
De Anza College
Cupertino, CA

Steven Rashba
University of Bridgeport
Bridgeport, CT

Mark Rau
American River College
Sacramento, CA

Maria Spelleri
State College of Florida
  Manatee-Sarasota
Venice, FL

Eva Teagarden
Yuba College
Marysville, CA

Colin S. Ward
Lone Star College-North
  Harris
Houston, TX

Nico Wiersema
Texas A&M International
  University
Laredo, TX

Susan Wilson
San Jose City College
San Jose, CA

A word from the author

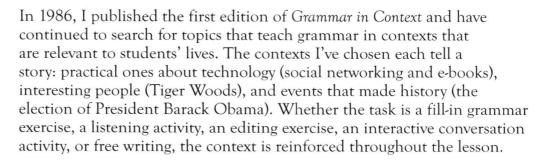

My parents immigrated to the U.S. from Poland and learned English as a second language. Born in the U.S., I often had the task as a child to explain the intricacies of the English language. It is no wonder that I became an English language teacher.

When I started teaching over forty years ago, grammar textbooks used a series of unrelated sentences with no context. I knew instinctively that there was something wrong with this technique. It ignored the fact that language is a tool for communication, and it missed an opportunity to spark the student's curiosity. As I gained teaching experience, I noticed that when I used interesting stories that illustrated the grammar, students became more motivated, understood the grammar better, and used it more effectively.

In 1986, I published the first edition of *Grammar in Context* and have continued to search for topics that teach grammar in contexts that are relevant to students' lives. The contexts I've chosen each tell a story: practical ones about technology (social networking and e-books), interesting people (Tiger Woods), and events that made history (the election of President Barack Obama). Whether the task is a fill-in grammar exercise, a listening activity, an editing exercise, an interactive conversation activity, or free writing, the context is reinforced throughout the lesson.

I hope you enjoy the new edition of *Grammar in Context!*

Sandra N. Elbaum

In memory of
Roberto Garrido Alfaro

Welcome to *Grammar in Context,*
Fifth Edition

Grammar in Context presents grammar in interesting contexts that are relevant to students' lives and then recycles the language and context throughout every activity. Learners gain knowledge and skills in both the grammar structures and topic areas.

The new fifth edition of *Grammar in Context* engages learners with updated readings, clear and manageable grammar explanations, and a new full-color design.

New To This Edition!

Full-color design makes grammar more visually contextualized and even easier to study and teach from.

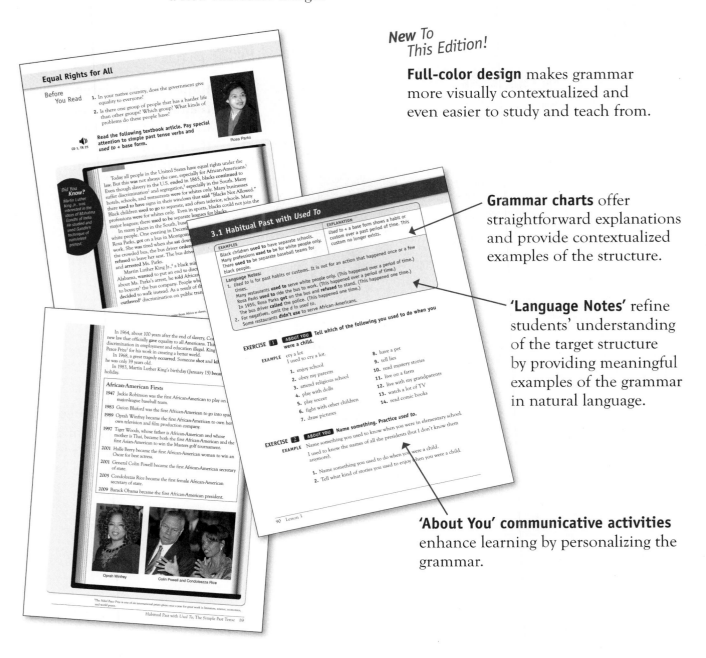

Grammar charts offer straightforward explanations and provide contextualized examples of the structure.

'Language Notes' refine students' understanding of the target structure by providing meaningful examples of the grammar in natural language.

'About You' communicative activities enhance learning by personalizing the grammar.

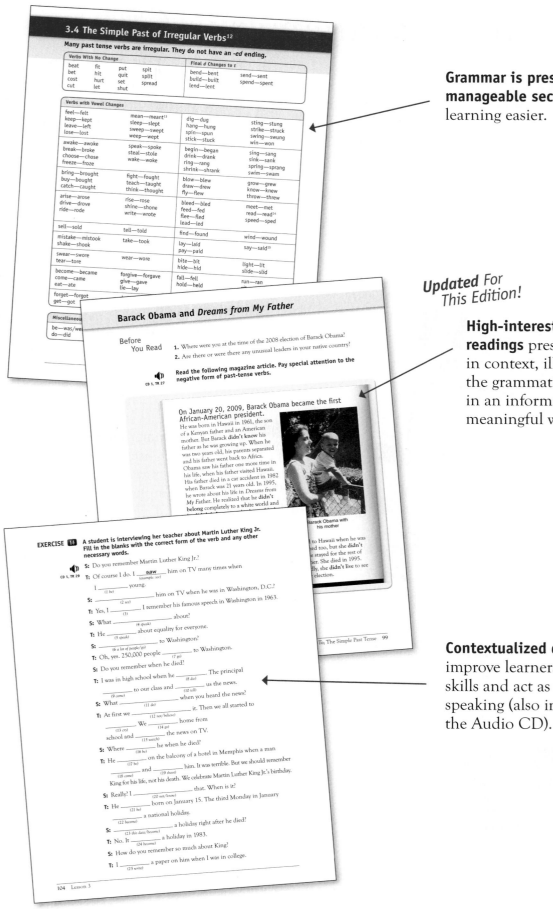

3.4 The Simple Past of Irregular Verbs[12]

Many past tense verbs are irregular. They do not have an -ed ending.

Verbs With No Change				Final d Changes to t	
beat	fit	put	spit	bend—bent	send—sent
bet	hit	quit	split	build—built	spend—spent
cost	hurt	set	spread	lend—lent	
cut	let	shut			

Verbs with Vowel Changes

feel—felt		dig—dug	sting—stung
keep—kept	mean—meant[13]	hang—hung	strike—struck
leave—left	sleep—slept	spin—spun	swing—swung
lose—lost	sweep—swept	stick—stuck	win—won
	weep—wept		
awake—awoke	speak—spoke	begin—began	sing—sang
break—broke	steal—stole	drink—drank	sink—sank
choose—chose	wake—woke	ring—rang	spring—sprang
freeze—froze		shrink—shrank	swim—swam
bring—brought	fight—fought	blow—blew	grow—grew
buy—bought	teach—taught	draw—drew	know—knew
catch—caught	think—thought	fly—flew	throw—threw
arise—arose	rise—rose	bleed—bled	meet—met
drive—drove	shine—shone	feed—fed	read—read[14]
ride—rode	write—wrote	flee—fled	speed—sped
		lead—led	
sell—sold	tell—told	find—found	
mistake—mistook	take—took	lay—laid	wind—wound
shake—shook		pay—paid	say—said[15]
swear—swore	wear—wore	bite—bit	light—lit
tear—tore		hide—hid	slide—slid
become—became	forgive—forgave	fall—fell	
come—came	give—gave	hold—held	run—ran
eat—ate	lie—lay		
forget—forgot			
get—got			

Miscellaneous

be—was/were
do—did

To; The Simple Past Tense   99

Barack Obama and *Dreams from My Father*

Before You Read

1. Where were you at the time of the 2008 election of Barack Obama?

2. Are there or were there any unusual leaders in your native country?

🔊 CD 1, TR 27   **Read the following magazine article. Pay special attention to the negative form of past-tense verbs.**

On January 20, 2009, Barack Obama became the first African-American president.

He was born in Hawaii in 1961, the son of a Kenyan father and an American mother. But Barack **didn't know** his father as he was growing up. When he was two years old, his parents separated and his father went back to Africa. Obama saw his father one more time in his life, when his father visited Hawaii. His father died in a car accident in 1982 when Barack was 21 years old. In 1995, he wrote about his life in *Dreams from My Father*. He realized that he **didn't belong** completely to a white world and

Barack Obama with his mother

...t to Hawaii when he was
...d too, but she **didn't**
...e stayed for the rest of
...er. She died in 1995.
...lly, she **didn't live** to see
... election.

EXERCISE **14**   A student is interviewing her teacher about Martin Luther King Jr. Fill in the blanks with the correct form of the verb and any other necessary words.

🔊 CD 1, TR 29

S: Do you remember Martin Luther King Jr.?

T: Of course I do. I ____**saw**____ (example: see) him on TV many times when I _____ (1 be) young.

S: _____ (2 see) him on TV when he was in Washington, D.C.?

T: Yes, I _____ (3) I remember his famous speech in Washington in 1963.

S: What _____ (4 speak) about?

T: He _____ (5 speak) about equality for everyone.

S: _____ (6 a lot of people/go) to Washington?

T: Oh, yes. 250,000 people _____ (7 go) to Washington.

S: Do you remember when he died?

T: I was in high school when he _____ (8 die) The principal _____ (9 come) to our class and _____ (10 tell) us the news.

S: What _____ (11 do) when you heard the news?

T: At first we _____ (12 not/believe) it. Then we all started to _____ (13 cry) We _____ (14 go) home from school and _____ (15 watch) the news on TV.

S: Where _____ (16 be) he when he died?

T: He _____ (17 be) on the balcony of a hotel in Memphis when a man _____ (18 come) and _____ (19 shoot) him. It was terrible. But we should remember King for his life, not his death. We celebrate Martin Luther King Jr.'s birthday.

S: Really? I _____ (20 not/know) that. When is it?

T: He _____ (21 be) born on January 15. The third Monday in January _____ (22 become) a national holiday.

S: _____ (23 this date/become) a holiday right after he died?

T: No. It _____ (24 become) a holiday in 1983.

S: How do you remember so much about King?

T: I _____ (25 write) a paper on him when I was in college.

Grammar is presented in clear, manageable sections to make learning easier.

Updated For This Edition!

High-interest, informative readings present grammar in context, illustrating the grammatical structure in an informative and meaningful way.

Contextualized dialogues improve learners' listening skills and act as models for speaking (also included on the Audio CD).

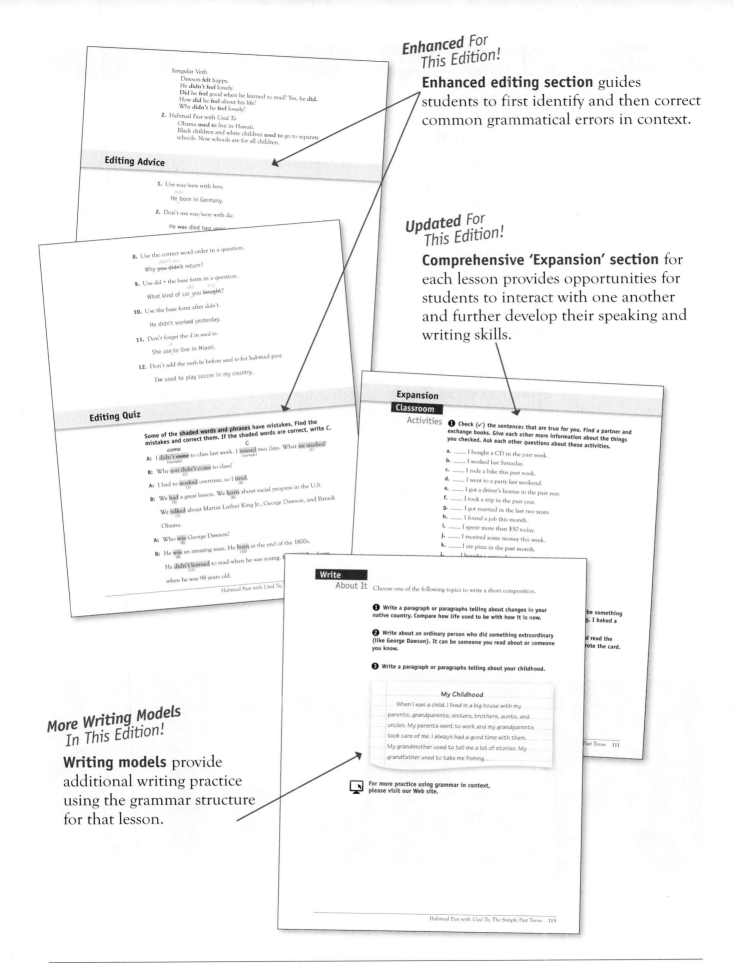

Enhanced For This Edition!

Enhanced editing section guides students to first identify and then correct common grammatical errors in context.

Updated For This Edition!

Comprehensive 'Expansion' section for each lesson provides opportunities for students to interact with one another and further develop their speaking and writing skills.

More Writing Models In This Edition!

Writing models provide additional writing practice using the grammar structure for that lesson.

Irregular Verb
Dawson **felt** happy.
He **didn't feel** lonely.
Did he **feel** good when he learned to read? Yes, he **did.**
How **did** he **feel** about his life?
Why **didn't** he **feel** lonely?

2. Habitual Past with *Used To*
Obama **used to** live in Hawaii.
Black children and white children **used to** go to separate schools. Now schools are for all children.

Editing Advice

1. Use *was/were* with *born*.
   He born in Germany.

2. Don't use *was/were* with *die*.
   He ~~was~~ died two years...

8. Use the correct word order in a question.
   Why ~~you didn't~~ return?

9. Use *did* + the base form in a question.
   What kind of car you ~~bought~~?

10. Use the base form after *didn't*.
    He didn't ~~worked~~ yesterday.

11. Don't forget the *d* in *used to*.
    She use to live in Miami.

12. Don't add the verb *be* before *used to* for habitual past.
    I'm used to play soccer in my country.

Editing Quiz

Some of the shaded words and phrases have mistakes. Find the mistakes and correct them. If the shaded words are correct, write *C*.

A: I didn't ~~came~~ to class last week. I missed two days. What we studied?

B: Why you didn't come to class?

A: I had to worked overtime, so I tired.

B: We had a great lesson. We learn about racial progress in the U.S.
We talked about Martin Luther King Jr., George Dawson, and Barack Obama.

A: Who was George Dawson?

B: He was an amazing man. He born at the end of the 1800s.
He didn't learned to read when he was young...learn when he was 98 years old.

Habitual Past with Used To;...

Expansion

Classroom Activities

❶ Check (✓) the sentences that are true for you. Find a partner and exchange books. Give each other more information about the things you checked. Ask each other questions about these activities.

a. ____ I bought a CD in the past week.
b. ____ I worked last Saturday.
c. ____ I rode a bike this past week.
d. ____ I went to a party last weekend.
e. ____ I got a driver's license in the past year.
f. ____ I took a trip in the past year.
g. ____ I got married in the last two years.
h. ____ I found a job this month.
i. ____ I spent more than $50 today.
j. ____ I received some money this week.
k. ____ I ate pizza in the past month.

Write

About It Choose one of the following topics to write a short composition.

❶ Write a paragraph or paragraphs telling about changes in your native country. Compare how life used to be with how it is now.

❷ Write about an ordinary person who did something extraordinary (like George Dawson). It can be someone you read about or someone you know.

❸ Write a paragraph or paragraphs telling about your childhood.

My Childhood
When I was a child, I lived in a big house with my parents, grandparents, sisters, brothers, aunts, and uncles. My parents went to work and my grandparents took care of me. I always had a good time with them. My grandmother used to tell me a lot of stories. My grandfather used to take me fishing...

For more practice using grammar in context, please visit our Web site.

Habitual Past with Used To; The Simple Past Tense 113

Additional resources for each level

FOR THE STUDENT:

New To *This Edition!*

- **Online Workbook** features additional exercises that learners can access in the classroom, language lab, or at home.

- **Audio CD** includes all readings and dialogues from the student book.

- Student Web site features additional practice: http://elt.heinle.com/ grammarincontext.

FOR THE TEACHER:

New To *This Edition!*

- **Online Lesson Planner** is perfect for busy instructors, allowing them to create and customize lesson plans for their classes, then save and share them in a range of formats.

Updated For *This Edition!*

- **Assessment CD-ROM with Exam*View*®** lets teachers create and customize tests and quizzes easily and includes many new contextualized test items.

- **Teacher's Edition** offers comprehensive teaching notes including suggestions for more streamlined classroom options.

- Instructor Web site includes a printable Student Book answer key.

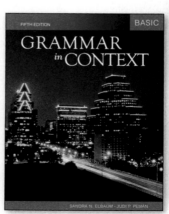 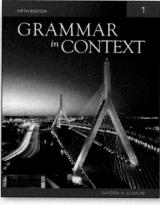 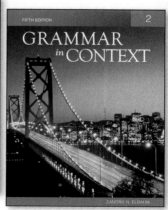 

Grammar
Modals

Related Expressions

Context
Renting an Apartment

8.1 Modals and Related Expressions—An Overview

A modal adds meaning to the verb that follows it.

List of Modals	Modals are different from other verbs in several ways.

can
could
should
will
would
may
might
must
	1. The base form of a verb follows a modal.[1]
	    You **must pay** your rent. (*Not:* You must <u>to</u> pay your rent.)
	    He **should clean** his apartment now. (*Not:* He should clean<u>ing</u> his apartment now.)
	
	2. Modals never have an *-s, -ed,* or *-ing* ending.
	    He **can** rent an apartment. (*Not:* He can<u>s</u> rent an apartment.)

Related Expressions	Some verbs are like modals in meaning.
have to be able to be supposed to be permitted/allowed to	He **must** sign the lease. = He **has to** sign the lease. He **can** pay the rent. = He **is able to** pay the rent. I **must** pay my rent by the first of the month. = I'**m supposed to** pay my rent by the first of the month. You **can't** change the locks in your apartment. = You **are not permitted to** change the locks in your apartment. = You **are not allowed to** change the locks in your apartment.

An Apartment Lease

Before You Read

1. Do you live in an apartment? Do you have a lease? Did you understand the lease when you signed it?

2. What kinds of things are not allowed in your apartment?

[1]Do not follow a modal with an infinitive. There is one exception: *ought to. Ought to* means *should.*

Read the following Web article. Pay special attention to modals and related expressions.

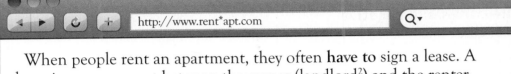

http://www.rent*apt.com

When people rent an apartment, they often **have to** sign a lease. A lease is an agreement between the owner (landlord[2]) and the renter (tenant). A lease states the period of time for the rental, the amount of the rent, and the rules the renter **must** follow. Some leases contain the following rules:

- Renters **must not** have a water bed.
- Renters **must not** have a pet.
- Renters **must not** change the locks without the owner's permission.
- Renters **must** pay a security deposit.

Many owners ask the renters to pay a security deposit in case there are damages. When the renters move out, the owners **are supposed to** return the deposit plus interest if the apartment is in good condition. If there is damage, the owners **can** use part or all of the money to repair the damage. However, they **may not** keep the renters' money for normal wear and tear (the normal use of the apartment).

Renters **do not have to** agree to all the terms of the lease. They **can** ask for changes before they sign. A pet owner, for example, **can** ask for permission to have a pet by offering to pay a higher security deposit.

There are laws that protect renters. For example, owners **must** provide heat during the winter months. In most cities, they **must** put a smoke detector in each apartment and in the halls. In addition, owners **can't** refuse to rent to a person because of sex, race, religion, nationality, or disability.

When the lease is up for renewal, owners **can** offer the renters a new lease or they **can** ask the renters to leave. The owners **are supposed to** notify the renters (usually at least 30 days in advance) if they want the renters to leave.

---

[2]A *landlord* is a man. A *landlady* is a woman.

8.2 Negatives with Modals

To form the negative of a modal, put *not* after the modal. You can make a negative contraction with some, but not all, modals.

Negatives and Negative Contractions	Examples
cannot → can't could not → couldn't should not → shouldn't will not → won't would not → wouldn't may not → (no contraction) might not → (no contraction) must not → mustn't	We **cannot** pay the rent. You **can't** have a dog in your apartment. We **will not** renew our lease. We **won't** stay here. You **may not** know legal terms. You **might not** understand the lease.
Language Note: Write *cannot* as one word.	

EXERCISE 1   **Write the negative form of the underlined words. Use a contraction whenever possible.**

EXAMPLE   You <u>must</u> pay a security deposit. You _____ **mustn't** _____ have a water bed.

1. I <u>can</u> have a cat in my apartment. I _____ *cann't* _____ have a dog.

2. You <u>should</u> read the lease carefully. You _____ *shouldn't* _____ sign it without reading it.

3. The landlord <u>must</u> install a smoke detector. You _____ *mustn't* _____ remove it.

4. You <u>may</u> have visitors in your apartment. You _____ *mayn't* _____ make a lot of noise and disturb your neighbors.

5. If you damage something, the landlord <u>can</u> keep part of your security deposit. He _____ *cann't* _____ keep your deposit without proof of damages.

6. You <u>might</u> get back all of your security deposit. If you leave your apartment in bad condition, you _____ *mightn't* _____ get all of it back.

8.3 Statements and Questions with Modals

Compare affirmative statements and questions with a modal.

Wh- Word	Modal	Subject	Modal	Verb (base form)	Complement	Short Answer
		He	**can**	have	a cat in his apartment.	
	Can	he		have	a water bed?	No, he **can't**.
What	**can**	he		have	in his apartment?	
		Who	**can**	have	a dog?	

Compare negative statements and questions with a modal.

Wh- Word	Modal	Subject	Modal	Verb (base form)	Complement
		He	**shouldn't**	pay	his rent late.
Why	**shouldn't**	he		pay	his rent late?

EXERCISE **2** **Read each statement. Fill in the blanks to complete the question.**

EXAMPLE You should read the lease before you sign it. Why _____ **should I** _(deber)_ read the lease before I sign it?

1. You can't have a water bed. Why _____ should I _____ a water bed?

2. We must pay a security deposit. How much _____ should We _____ ?

3. Someone must install a smoke detector. Who _____ should it _____ a smoke detector?

4. The landlord can't refuse to rent to a person because of race, religion, or nationality. Why _____ should _____ to rent to a person for these reasons?

5. Tenants shouldn't make a lot of noise in their apartments. Why _____ should _____ a lot of noise?

6. I may have a cat in my apartment. _____ I should _____ have a dog in my apartment?

7. The landlord can have a key to my apartment. _____ He _____ _____ enter my apartment when I'm not home?

8.4 Must, Have To, Have Got To

The modal *must* has a very official tone. For nonofficial situations, we usually use *have to* or *have got to*.

EXAMPLES	EXPLANATION
The landlord **must** give you a smoke detector. The tenant **must** pay the rent on the first of each month.	For formal obligations, use *must*. *Must* is often used in legal contracts, such as apartment leases.
The landlord **has to** give you a smoke detector. The landlord **has got to** give you a smoke detector.	We can also use *have to* or *have got to*, for obligations.
You **must** leave the building immediately. It's on fire! You **have to** leave the building immediately. It's on fire! You**'ve got to** leave the building immediately. It's on fire!	*Must, have to,* and *have got to* express a sense of urgency. All three sentences to the left have the same meaning. *Have got to* is usually contracted: I have got to = I've got to He has got to = He's got to
Our apartment is too small. We **have to** move. Our apartment is too small. We**'ve got to** move.	Avoid using *must* for personal obligations. It sounds very official or urgent and is too strong for most situations. Use *have to* or *have got to*.
At the end of my lease last May, I **had to** move. I **had to** find a bigger apartment.	*Must* has no past form. The past of both *must* and *have to* is *had to*. *Have got to* has no past form.

Language Note: We don't usually use *have got to* for questions and negatives.
Pronunciation Note: In fast, informal speech, *have to* is often pronounced "hafta." *Has to* is often pronounced "hasta." *Got to* is often pronounced "gotta." Often *have* is omitted before "gotta." Listen to your teacher pronounce the sentences in the above chart.

EXERCISE 3 **Fill in the blanks with an appropriate verb. Answers may vary.**

EXAMPLE   The landlord must __*provide*__ heat in cold weather.

1. You must _____ the lease with a pen. A pencil is not acceptable.

2. The landlord must _____ your security deposit if you leave your apartment in good condition.

3. The landlord must _____ you if he wants you to leave at the end of your lease.

4. You must _____ quiet in your apartment at night. Neighbors want to sleep.

EXERCISE 4 **ABOUT YOU** Make a list of personal obligations you have.

EXAMPLE I have to help my parents on the weekend.

1. _I have to clean my apartment every saturday._
2. _I have to go to market each sunday._
3. _I have to washin my clothes every weekend._

EXERCISE 5 **ABOUT YOU** Make a list of things you had to do last weekend.

EXAMPLE I had to do my laundry.

1. _I had_
2. _I had_
3. _I had_

EXERCISE 6 Finish these statements. Practice *have got to*. Answers will vary.

EXAMPLE When you live in the U.S., you've got to _learn English._

1. When I don't know the meaning of a word, I've got to _____

_____

2. English is so important in the U.S. We've got to _____

_____

3. For this class, you've got to _____

_____

4. If you rent an apartment, you've got to _____

_____

5. If you want to drive a car, you've got to _____

_____

8.5 Obligation with *Must* or *Be Supposed To*

EXAMPLES	EXPLANATION
Landlord to tenant: "You **must** pay your rent on the first of each month." Judge to landlord: "You have no proof of damage. You **must** return the security deposit to your tenant."	*Must* has an official, formal tone. A person in a position of authority (like a landlord or judge) can use *must*.
Wording on a lease: The tenant **must not** change the locks.	Legal documents use *must*.
You**'re supposed to** put your name on your mailbox. The landlord **is supposed to** give you a copy of the lease.	Avoid using *must* if you are not in a position of authority. Use *be supposed to*.
We**'re not supposed to** have cats in my building, but my neighbor has one. The landlord **was supposed to** return my security deposit, but he didn't. I**'m supposed to** pay my rent on the first of the month, but sometimes I forget.	*Be supposed to*, not *must*, is used when reporting on a law or rule that was broken or a task that wasn't completed.

Pronunciation Note: The *d* in *supposed to* is usually not pronounced.

EXERCISE 7   **Make these sentences less formal by changing from *must* to *be supposed to*.**

EXAMPLE   You must wear your seat belt.
You're supposed to wear your seat belt.

1. You must carry your driver's license with you when you drive.
2. You must stop at a red light.
3. We must put money in the parking meter during business hours.
4. Your landlord must notify you if he wants you to leave.
5. The landlord must give me a smoke detector.
6. The teacher must give a final grade at the end of the semester.
7. We must write five compositions in this course.
8. We must bring our books to class.

EXERCISE 8 Finish these statements. Use *be supposed to* plus a verb. Answers may vary.

EXAMPLE I _'m supposed to pay my rent_____ on the first of the month.

1. Pets are not permitted in my apartment. I (not) _____ a pet.

2. The landlord _____ heat in the winter months.

3. The tenants _____ before they move out.

4. The landlord _____ a smoke detector in each apartment.

5. I _____ my rent last week, but I forgot.

6. My stove isn't working. My landlord _____ it.

7. We're going to move out next week. Our apartment is clean and in good condition. The landlord _____ our security deposit.

8. The janitor _____ the garbage every day.

9. The janitor _____ the hallway twice a week.

10. When we move furniture, we _____ the back stairs, not the front stairs.

EXERCISE 9 **ABOUT YOU** Write three sentences to tell what you are supposed to do for this course. You may work with a partner.

EXAMPLE _We're supposed to write three compositions this semester._____

1. _____

_____

2. _____

_____

3. _____

_____

8.6 Can, May, Could, and Alternate Expressions

EXAMPLE WITH A MODAL	ALTERNATE EXPRESSION	EXPLANATION
I **can** clean the apartment by Friday.	It **is possible** (for me) **to** clean the apartment by Friday.	Possibility
I **can't** understand the lease.	I **am not able to** understand the lease.	Ability
I **can't** have a pet in my apartment.	I **am not permitted to** have a pet. I **am not allowed to** have a pet.	Permission
The landlord **may not** keep my deposit if my apartment is clean and in good condition.	The landlord **is not permitted to** keep my deposit. The landlord **is not allowed to** keep my deposit.	Permission
I **couldn't** speak English five years ago, but I can now.	I **wasn't able to** speak English five years ago, but I can now.	Past Ability
I **could** have a dog in my last apartment, but I can't have one in my present apartment.	I **was permitted to** have a dog in my last apartment, but I can't have one in my present apartment.	Past Permission

Language Note: We use *can* in the following common expression:
I *can't afford* a bigger apartment. I don't have enough money.

Pronunciation Note: *Can* is not usually stressed in affirmative statements. In negative statements, *can't* is stressed but it is hard to hear the final *t*. So we must pay attention to the vowel sound to hear the difference between *can* and *can't*. Listen to your teacher pronounce these sentences:

I can gó. /kIn/
I cán't go. /kænt/

In a short answer, we pronounce *can* as /kæn/.
Can you help me later?
Yes, I can. /kæn/

EXERCISE **10** **Fill in the blanks with an appropriate permission word to talk about what is or isn't permitted at this school. Answers may vary.**

EXAMPLES   We ___aren't allowed to___ bring food into the classroom.

We _____can_____ leave the room without asking the teacher for permission.

1. We _____ eat in the classroom.
2. Students _____ talk during a test.

3. Students _____ use their dictionaries when they write composition.

4. Students _____ write a test with a pencil.

5. Students _____ sit in any seat they want.

6. Students _____ use their textbooks during a test.

EXERCISE 11 **Complete each statement. Answers may vary.**

EXAMPLES   The landlord may not ___refuse to rent___ to a person because of his or her nationality.

The tenants may ___use___ the washing machines in the basement.

1. The tenants may not _____ the locks without the landlord's permission.

2. Each tenant in my building has a parking space. I may not _____ in another tenant's space.

3. Students may not _____ during a test.

4. Teacher to students: "You don't need my permission to leave the room. You may _____ the room if you need to."

5. Some teachers do not allow cell phones in class. In Mr. Klein's class, you may not _____ during class.

6. My teacher says that after we finish a test, we may _____. We don't have to stay in class.

EXERCISE 12 **ABOUT YOU** **Write statements to tell what is or is not permitted in this class, in the library, at this school, or during a test. If you have any questions about what is permitted, write a question for the teacher. You may work with a partner.**

EXAMPLES   We aren't allowed to talk in the library.

May we use our textbooks during a test?

_____

_____

_____

_____

_____

EXERCISE **13**   **ABOUT YOU** Write three sentences telling about what you couldn't do in another class or school that you attended.

EXAMPLE   In my school, I couldn't call a teacher by his first name,

but I can do it here.

1. _____

_____

2. _____

_____

3. _____

_____

EXERCISE **14**   **ABOUT YOU** If you come from another country, write three sentences telling about something that was prohibited there that you can do in the U.S.

EXAMPLE   I couldn't criticize the political leaders in my country,

but I can do it in the U.S.

1. _____

_____

2. _____

_____

3. _____

_____

Tenants' Rights

Before
You Read

1. What are some complaints you have about your apartment? Do you ever tell the landlord about your complaints?

2. Is your apartment warm enough in the winter and cool enough in the summer?

CD 3, TR 02

Read the following conversation. Pay special attention to *should* and *had better*.

A: My apartment is always too cold in the winter. I've got to move.

B: You don't have to move. The landlord is supposed to provide enough heat.

A: But he doesn't.

B: You **should** talk to him about this problem.

A: I did already. The first time I talked to him, he just told me I **should** put on a sweater. The second time I said, "You**'d better** give me heat, or I'm going to move."

B: You **shouldn't** get so angry. That's not the way to solve the problem. You know, there are laws about heat. You **should** get information from the city so you can know your rights.

A: How can I get information?

B: You **should** go online and get information about tenants' rights from the city's Web site. When you know exactly what the law is, you **should** present this information to your landlord.

A: And what if he doesn't want to do anything about it?

B: Then you **should** report the problem to the mayor's office.

A: I'm afraid to do that.

B: Don't be afraid. You have rights. Maybe you **should** talk to other tenants and see if you can do this together.

8.7 Should; Had Better

EXAMPLES	EXPLANATION

You **should** talk to the landlord about the problem.
You **should** get information about tenants' rights.
You **shouldn't** get so angry.
	For advice, use *should*.
	   Should = It's a good idea.
	   Shouldn't = It's a bad idea.

Compare: Your landlord **must** give you a smoke detector. You **should** check the battery in the smoke detector occasionally.	Remember, *must* is very strong and is not for advice. It is for rules and laws. For advice, use *should*.
You **had better** give me heat, or I'm going to move. We**'d better not** make so much noise, or our neighbors will complain.	For a warning, use *had better (not)*. Something bad can happen if you don't follow this advice. The contraction for *had* (in *had better*) is *'d*. I'd you'd he'd she'd we'd they'd

Pronunciation Note:
Native speakers often don't pronounce the *had* or *'d* in *had better*. You will hear people say,
   "**You better** be quiet; **you better** not make so much noise."

EXERCISE 15   **Give advice using *should*. Answers will vary.**

EXAMPLE   I'm going to move next week, and I hope to get my security deposit back.
Advice: <u>You should clean the apartment completely.</u>

1. I just rented an apartment, but the rent is too high for me alone.
Advice: _____

2. My upstairs neighbors make a lot of noise.
Advice: _____

3. The battery in the smoke detector is old.
Advice: _____

4. I want to paint the walls.
Advice: _____

5. The rent was due last week, but I forgot to pay it.
Advice: _____

6. My landlady doesn't provide enough heat in the winter.
Advice: _____

7. I can't understand my lease.

Advice: _____

8. I broke a window in my apartment.

Advice: _____

9. My landlord doesn't want to return my security deposit.

Advice: _____

10. The landlord is going to raise the rent by 40 percent.

Advice: _____

EXERCISE 16 **Fill in the blanks with an appropriate verb (phrase) to complete this conversation. Answers may vary.**

A: My mother is such a worrier.

CD 3, TR 03

B: What does she worry about?

A: Everything. Especially me.

B: For example?

A: Even if it's warm outside, she always says, "you'd better ___take a sweater___ because it might get cold later," or "You'd
(example)

better _____ because it might rain." When I drive,
_(1)_

she always tells me, "You'd better _____, or you might
_(2)_

get a ticket." If I stay out late with my friends, she tells me, "You'd

better _____, or you won't get enough sleep." If I read
_(3)_

a lot, she says, "You'd better not _____, or you'll ruin
_(4)_

your eyesight."

B: Well, she's your mother. So naturally she worries about you.

A: But she worries about other things too.

B: Like what?

A: "You'd better _____ your shoes when you enter the
_(5)_

apartment, or the neighbors downstairs will hear us walking around.

We'd better _____, or the neighbors will complain
_(6)_

about the noise in our apartment."

B: It sounds like she's a good neighbor.

(continued)

Modals; Related Expressions   253

A: That's not all. She unplugs the TV every night. She says, "I'd better

_____, or the apartment will fill up with radiation."
(7)

And she doesn't want to use a cell phone. She says it has too much

radiation. I think that's so silly.

B: I don't think that's silly. You'd better _____ some
(8)

articles about cell phones, because they do produce radiation.

A: I don't even use my cell phone very much. But my mother always tells

me, "You'd better _____ in case I need to call you."
(9)

B: Do you live with your mother?

A: Yes, I do. I think I'd better _____ to my own
(10)

apartment, or she'll drive me crazy.

Using Craigslist.org to Find a Roommate

Before
You Read

1. Do you ever use the Internet to find an apartment?

2. How did you find your current apartment?

Read the following conversation. Pay special attention to the negative of modals and related expressions.

A: I'm looking for a new roommate. My roommate moved out last month, and I **can't** pay the rent by myself.

B: You can put an ad on Craigslist.

A: What's that?

B: It's a Web site where you can advertise. You can sell, buy, rent, find jobs, look for roommates—you can do a lot of things on Craigslist.org.

A: How much does it cost to put an ad on this site?

B: It's free. You **don't have to** pay anything. Let's go to the computer. I'll show you. . . . *[looking at the Web site]*

A: These ads all have pictures.

B: You **don't have to** include pictures, but it's a good idea. You get more responses if you include pictures.

A: This is great. Can you help me write an ad?

B: Sure. You included your phone number.

A: What's wrong with that?

B: You **shouldn't** include it. It's better if you get e-mail.

A: OK. Now let's take pictures of my apartment. I'll get my camera.

B: You'd **better not** take pictures yet. Your apartment is a mess. You need to clean it up first.

A: Oh, right.

B: You know, I just thought of something. My cousin, Lisa, needs a roommate.

A: Lisa? She has a dog. We **can't** have dogs in the apartment.

B: Are you sure? Look at your lease.

A: Here it is. It says, "Renters **may not** have a pet." Besides, Lisa's a woman. In my country, men and women **aren't supposed to** live together. My parents wouldn't like it.

B: They **don't have to** know. They don't even live in this country.

A: I'd **better not** do it. I can't lie to my parents.

8.8 Negatives of Modals

EXAMPLES	EXPLANATION
Renters **may not** have a pet. Renters **must not** change the locks without the owner's permission.	Prohibition in documents is often expressed with *may not* or *must not*. These modals sound very formal or official.
a. I **can't** have a dog in my apartment. a. We **can't** leave our bikes in the hallway. b. I **can't** pay the rent by myself. b. I **can't** carry my bike up the stairs. It's too heavy.	a. *Cannot*, in these examples, shows prohibition. It is less formal than *may not* or *must not*. b. *Cannot*, in these examples, shows inability.
a. You**'re not supposed to** have a dog in your apartment. b. In my country, men and women **are not supposed to** live together if they're not married.	a. *You're not supposed to* is a less formal way of showing prohibition than *you may not*. b. *Be not supposed to*, in this example, shows a custom.
You **shouldn't** include your phone number in the ad. In case of fire, you **shouldn't** use the elevator. You **shouldn't** leave your door unlocked. It's not safe.	*Shouldn't* gives advice.
a. You**'d better not** take pictures now. Your apartment is a mess. b. I**'d better not** get a female roommate. My parents wouldn't like it.	a. *Had better not* is used for a warning. b. *Had better not* can be an emotional response to a suggestion to do something wrong.
a. You **don't have to** tell your parents. b. You **don't have to** include pictures on Craigslist, but it's a good idea.	a. *Don't have to* means not necessary. b. *Don't have to* sometimes means that you have an option (include picture or not).
Compare: a. We**'re not supposed to** leave our bikes near the door, but someone always does it. b. You **shouldn't** lie to your parents. c. You **don't have to** include pictures on Craigslist. It's your choice. d. Tenants **must not** change the locks.	Sentence (a) shows that a rule is violated. Sentence (b) gives advice. Sentence (c) shows that something is not necessary. Sentence (d) shows that something is not permitted. In affirmative statements, *must* and *have to* have very similar meanings. However, in negative statements, the meaning is very different: • not have to = not necessary • must not = prohibited

EXERCISE 17 Practice using *must not* for prohibition. Use *you* in the impersonal sense. Answers will vary.

EXAMPLE Name something you must not do.
You must not steal.

1. Name something you must not do on the bus.
2. Name something you mustn't do during a test.
3. Name something you mustn't do in the library.
4. Name something you must not do in the classroom.
5. Name something you mustn't do on an airplane.

EXERCISE 18 **ABOUT YOU** Tell if you *have to* or *don't have to* do the following. For affirmative statements, you can also use *have got to*.

EXAMPLES work on Saturdays
I have to work on Saturdays. OR I've got to work on Saturdays.

wear a suit to work
I don't have to wear a suit to work.

1. speak English every day
2. use a dictionary to read the newspaper
3. pay rent on the first of the month
4. type my homework
5. work on Saturdays
6. come to school every day
7. pay my rent in cash
8. use public transportation
9. talk to the teacher after class
10. cook every day

EXERCISE 19 Ask a student who comes from another country these questions.

1. In your native country, does a citizen have to vote?
2. Do men have to serve in the military?
3. Do schoolchildren have to wear uniforms?
4. Do people have to get permission to travel?
5. Do students have to pass an exam to get their high school or university diploma?

6. Do students have to pay for their own books?

7. Do citizens have to pay taxes?

8. Do people have to make an appointment to see a doctor?

EXERCISE 20 **Fill in the blanks with _be not supposed to_ (when there is a rule) or _don't have to_ (when something is not necessary).**

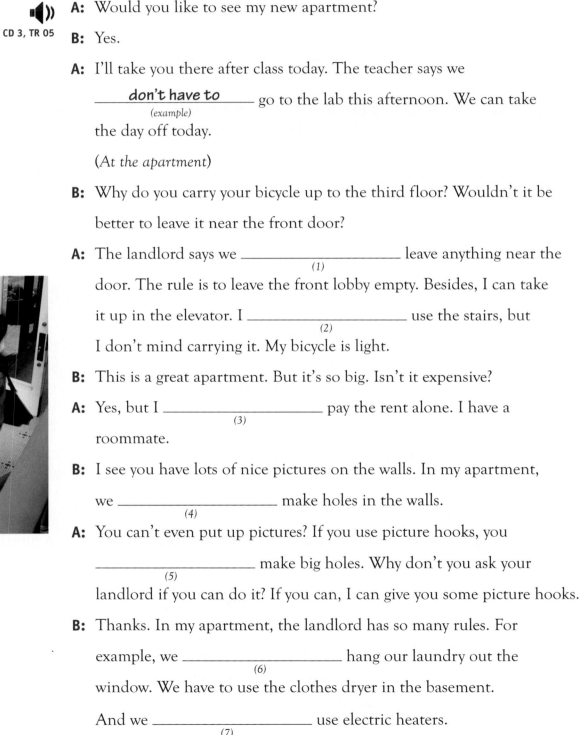

CD 3, TR 05

A: Would you like to see my new apartment?

B: Yes.

A: I'll take you there after class today. The teacher says we

_____**don't have to**_____ go to the lab this afternoon. We can take
(example)
the day off today.

(*At the apartment*)

B: Why do you carry your bicycle up to the third floor? Wouldn't it be

better to leave it near the front door?

A: The landlord says we _____(1)_____ leave anything near the

door. The rule is to leave the front lobby empty. Besides, I can take

it up in the elevator. I _____(2)_____ use the stairs, but

I don't mind carrying it. My bicycle is light.

B: This is a great apartment. But it's so big. Isn't it expensive?

A: Yes, but I _____(3)_____ pay the rent alone. I have a

roommate.

B: I see you have lots of nice pictures on the walls. In my apartment,

we _____(4)_____ make holes in the walls.

A: You can't even put up pictures? If you use picture hooks, you

_____(5)_____ make big holes. Why don't you ask your

landlord if you can do it? If you can, I can give you some picture hooks.

B: Thanks. In my apartment, the landlord has so many rules. For

example, we _____(6)_____ hang our laundry out the

window. We have to use the clothes dryer in the basement.

And we _____(7)_____ use electric heaters.

A: An electric heater can sometimes cause a fire. I'm sure the apartment has heaters for each room. And in the U.S. people don't usually hang clothes to dry out the window. People use dryers.

B: There are so many different rules and customs here.

A: Don't worry. If you do something wrong, someone will tell you.

EXERCISE **21** Students (S) are asking the teacher (T) questions about the final exam. Fill in the blanks with the negative form of *have to, should, must, had better, can, may,* or *be supposed to*. In some cases, more than one answer is possible.

CD 3, TR 06

S: Do I have to sit in a specific seat for the test?

T: No, you ____don't have to____. You can choose any seat you want.
(example)

S: Is it OK if I talk to another student during a test?

T: No. Absolutely not. You _____ talk to another
(1)
student during a test.

S: Is it OK if I use my book?

T: Sorry. You _____ use your book.
(2)

S: What if I don't understand something on the test? Can I ask another student?

T: You _____ talk to another student, or I'll think
(3)
you're getting an answer. Ask me if you have a question.

S: What happens if I'm late for the test? Will you let me in?

T: Of course I'll let you in. But you _____ come late.
(4)
You'll need a lot of time for the test.

S: Do I have to bring my own paper for the final test?

T: If you want to, you can. But you _____ bring paper.
(5)
I'll give you paper if you need it.

S: Must I use a pen?

T: You can use whatever you want. You _____ use a pen.
(6)

S: Do you have any advice on test-taking?

(continued)

T: Yes. If you see an item that is difficult for you, go on to the next item. You _____ spend too much time on a difficult item, or you won't finish the test.
(7)

S: Can I bring coffee into the classroom?

T: The school has a rule about eating or drinking in the classroom. You _____ bring food or drinks into the classroom.
(8)

S: If I finish the test early, must I stay in the room?

T: No, you _____ stay. You can leave.
(9)

The New Neighbors

Before You Read

1. Are people friendly with their neighbors in your community?

2. Do you know any of your neighbors now?

Read the following conversation. Pay special attention to *must*.

> *Lisa (L) knocks on the door of her new upstairs neighbor, Paula (P).*

L: Hi. You **must be** the new neighbor. I saw the moving truck out front this morning. Let me introduce myself. My name is Lisa. I live downstairs from you.

P: Nice to meet you, Lisa. My name is Paula. We just moved in.

L: I saw the movers carrying a crib upstairs. You **must have** a baby.

P: We do. We have a 10-month-old son. He's sleeping now. Do you have any kids?

L: Yes. I have a 16-year-old-daughter and an 18-year-old son.

P: It **must be** hard to raise teenagers.

L: Believe me, it is! I **must spend** half my time worrying about where they are and what they're doing. My daughter talks on the phone all day. She **must spend** half of her waking hours on the phone with her friends. They're always whispering to each other. They **must have** some big secrets.

P: I know what you mean. My brother has a teenage daughter.

L: Listen, I don't want to take up any more of your time. You **must be** very busy. I just wanted to bring you these cookies.

P: Thanks. That's very nice of you. They're still warm. They **must be** right out of the oven.

L: They are. Maybe we can talk some other time when you're all unpacked.

8.9 *Must* for Conclusions

In Section 8.4, we studied *must* to express necessity. *Must* has another use: we use it to show a logical conclusion or deduction based on information we have or observations we make. *Must*, in this case, is for the present only, not the future.

EXAMPLES	EXPLANATION
a. The new neighbors have a crib. They **must have** a baby.	a. You see the crib, so you conclude that they have a baby.
b. Paula just moved in. She **must be** very busy.	b. You know how hard it is to move, so you conclude that she is busy.
c. The teenage girls whisper all the time. They **must have** secrets.	c. You see them whispering, so you conclude that they are telling secrets.
I didn't see Paula's husband. He **must not be** home.	For a negative deduction, use *must not*. Do not use a contraction.

EXERCISE 22 **A week later, Paula goes to Lisa's apartment and notices certain things. Use *must* + base form to show Paula's conclusions about Lisa's life. Answers may vary.**

EXAMPLE   There is a bowl of food on the kitchen floor.
<u>Lisa must have a pet.</u>

1. There are pictures of Lisa and her two children all over the house. There is no picture of a man.

   _____

2. There is a nursing certificate on the wall with Lisa's name on it.

   _____

3. There are many different kinds of coffee on a kitchen shelf.

   _____

4. There are a lot of classical music CDs.

   _____

5. In Lisa's bedroom, there's a sewing machine.

   _____

6. In the kitchen, there are a lot of cookbooks.

   _____

7. There's a piano in the living room.

   _____

8. On the bookshelf, there are a lot of books about modern art.

   _____

9. On the kitchen calendar, there's an activity filled in for almost every day of the week.

   _____

10. There are pictures of cats everywhere.

   _____

EXERCISE 23 **Two neighbors, Alma (A) and Eva (E), meet in the hallway of their building. Fill in the blanks with an appropriate verb to show deduction.**

CD 3, TR 08

A: Hi. My name's Alma. I live on the third floor. You must

   _____<u>be</u>_____ new in this building.
      (example)

E: I am. We just moved in last week. My name's Eva.

A: I noticed your last name on the mailbox. It's Kovič. That sounds like a Bosnian name. You must _____ from Bosnia.
(1)

E: I am. How did you know?

A: I'm from Bosnia too. Did you come directly to the U.S. from Bosnia?

E: No. I stayed in Germany for three years.

A: Then you must _____ German.
(2)

E: I can speak it pretty well, but I can't write it well.

A: Are you going to school now?

E: Yes, I'm taking English classes at Washington College.

A: What level are you in?

E: I'm in Level 5.

A: Then you must _____ my husband. He takes classes there too.
(3)
He's in Level 5 too.

E: There's only one guy with a Bosnian last name. That must
_____ your husband.
(4)

A: His name is Hasan.

E: Oh, yes, I know him. I didn't know he lived in the same building. I never see him here. He must not _____ home very much.
(5)

A: He isn't. He has two jobs.

E: Do you take English classes?

A: Not anymore. I came here 15 years ago.

E: Then your English must _____ perfect.
(6)

A: I don't know if it's perfect, but it's good enough.

8.10 Will and May/Might

EXAMPLES	EXPLANATION
My lease **will** expire on April 30. We **won't** sign another lease.	For certainty about the future, use *will*. The negative contraction for *will not* is *won't*.
a. My landlord **might** raise my rent at that time. a. I **may** move. b. I don't know what "tenant" means. Let's ask the teacher. She **might** know. b. The teacher **may** have information about tenants' rights.	*May* and *might* both have about the same meaning: possibility or uncertainty. a. about the future b. about the present
He **may not** renew our lease. He **might not** renew our lease.	We don't use a contraction for *may not* and *might not*.
Compare: a. **Maybe** I will move. b. I **might** move. a. **Maybe** he doesn't understand the lease. b. He **might** not understand the lease. a. **Maybe** the apartment is cold in winter. (*maybe* = adverb) b. The apartment **may** be cold in winter. (*may + be* = modal + verb)	*Maybe* is an adverb. It is one word. It usually comes at the beginning of the sentence and means *possibly* or *perhaps*. *May* and *might* are modals. They follow the subject and precede the verb. Sentences (a) and (b) have the same meaning. *Wrong:* I *maybe* will move. *Wrong:* He *maybe* doesn't understand. *Wrong:* The apartment *maybe* is cold.

EXERCISE 24 The following sentences contain *maybe*. Take away *maybe* and use *may* or *might* + base form.

EXAMPLE Maybe your neighbors will complain if your music is loud.
Your neighbors might complain if your music is loud.

1. Maybe my sister will come to live with me.

2. Maybe she will find a job in this city.

3. Maybe my landlord will raise my rent.

4. Maybe I will get a dog.

5. Maybe my landlord won't allow me to have a dog.

6. Maybe I will move next year.

7. Maybe I will buy a house soon.

8. Maybe I won't stay in this city.

9. Maybe I won't come to class tomorrow.

10. Maybe the teacher will review modals if we need more help.

EXERCISE 25 **ABOUT YOU** **Fill in the blanks with a possibility.**

EXAMPLES   If I don't pay my rent on time, _I might have to pay a late fee._

If I make a lot of noise in my apartment, _the neighbors may complain._

1. When my lease is up, _____

2. If I don't clean my apartment before I move out, _____

_____

3. If I don't study for the next test, _____

4. If we don't register for classes early, _____

_____

5. If I don't pass this course, _____

EXERCISE 26 **Fill in the blanks with possibilities. Answers may vary.**

EXAMPLE   **A:** I'm going to move on Saturday. I might ___need___ help. Can you

help me?

🔊
CD 3, TR 09   **B:** I'm not sure. I may ___go___ to the country with my family if the

weather is nice. If I stay here, I'll help you.

1. **A:** My next door neighbor's name is Terry Karson. I see her name on

the doorbell but I never see her.

B: Why do you say "her"? Your neighbor may _____ a man.

Terry is sometimes a man's name.

2. **A:** I need coins for the laundry room. Do you have any?

B: Let me look. I might _____ some. No, I don't have any. Look in

the laundry room. There might _____ a dollar-bill changer there.

3. **A:** Do you know the landlord's address?

B: No, I don't. Ask the manager. She might _____.

A: Where's the manager now?

B: I'm not sure. She might _____ in a tenant's apartment.

4. **A:** Do they allow cats in this building?

B: I'm not sure. I know they don't allow dogs, but they might

_____ cats.

(continued)

5. **A:** We'd better close the windows before going out.

   B: Why? It's a hot day today.

   A: Look how gray the sky is. It might _____.

6. **A:** Are you going to stay in this apartment for another year?

   B: I'm not sure. I may _____.

   A: Why?

   B: The landlord might _____ the rent. If the rent goes up more than 25 percent, I'll move.

7. **A:** I have so much stuff in my closet. There's not enough room for my clothes.

   B: There might _____ lockers in the basement where you can store your things.

   A: Really? I didn't know that.

   B: Let's look. I may _____ a key to the basement with me.

   A: That would be great.

   B: Hmm. I don't have one on me. Let's go to my apartment. My basement keys might _____ there.

At A Garage Sale

Before You Read

1. People often have a garage sale or yard sale or an apartment sale before they move. At this kind of sale, people sell things that they don't want or need anymore. Do you ever go to garage sales?

2. At a garage or yard sale, it is usually not necessary to pay the asking price. You may be able to bargain[3] with the seller. Can you bargain the price in other places?

---

[3]When a buyer *bargains* with the seller, the buyer makes an offer lower than the asking price and hopes that he or she and the seller will agree on a lower price.

CD 3, TR 10

This is a conversation at a garage sale between a seller (S) and a buyer (B). Read the conversation. Pay special attention to modals and related expressions.

S: I see you're looking at my microwave oven. **May** I answer any questions?

B: Yes. I'm interested in buying one. Does it work well?

S: It's only two years old, and it's in perfect working condition. **Would** you **like** to try it out?

B: Sure. **Could** you plug it in somewhere?

S: I have an outlet right here. **Why don't we** boil a cup of water so you can see how well it works?

(*A few minutes later*)

B: It seems to work well. **Would** you tell me why you're selling it, then?

S: We're moving next week. Our new apartment already has one.

B: How much do you want for it?[4]

S: $40.

B: **Will** you take $30?

S: **Can** you wait a minute? I'll ask my wife.

(*A few minutes later*)

S: My wife says she'll let you have it for $35.

B: OK. **May** I write you a check?

S: I'm sorry. I'**d rather** have cash.

B: **Would** you hold it for me for an hour? I can go to the ATM[5] and get cash.

S: **Could** you leave me a small deposit? Ten dollars, maybe?

B: Yes, I can.

S: Fine. I'll hold it for you.

[4]We ask "How much is it?" when the price is fixed. We ask "How much do you want for it?" when the price is negotiable—you can bargain for it.

[5]An *ATM* is an Automatic Teller Machine. You can use this machine to get cash from your bank account.

8.11 Using Modals and Questions for Politeness

	EXAMPLES	EXPLANATION
To ask permission	**May** **Can** **Could** } I write you a check?	*May* and *could* are considered more polite than *can* by some speakers of English.
To request that someone do something	**Can** **Could** **Will** **Would** } you plug it in?	For a request, *could* and *would* are softer than *can* and *will*.
To express want or desire	**Would** you **like** to try out the microwave oven? Yes, I **would like** to see if it works. I**'d like** to boil a cup of water.	*Would like* has the same meaning as *want*. *Would like* is softer than *want*. The contraction for *would* after a pronoun is *'d*.
To express preference	I **would rather** buy a used microwave **than** a new one. **Would** you **rather** pay with cash **or** by check? I**'d rather** pay by check.	Use *than* in statements with *would rather* to show options. Use *or* in questions. The second option can be omitted if it's obvious.
To offer a suggestion	**Why don't you** go to the ATM to get cash? **Why don't we** boil a cup of water? **Compare:** Go to the ATM. Boil a cup of water.	We can make a suggestion more polite by using a negative question.

Language Note: Modals and questions are often used to make direct statements more polite.
Compare:
    Plug it in. (very direct)
    Would you plug it in? (more polite)

EXERCISE **27**   **Change each request to make it more polite. Practice *may*, *can*, and *could* + I.**

EXAMPLES   I want to use your phone.
May I use your phone?

I want to borrow a quarter.
Could I borrow a quarter?

    1. I want to help you.
    2. I want to close the door.
    3. I want to leave the room.
    4. I want to write you a check.

EXERCISE 28 **Change these commands to make them more polite. Practice *can you*, *could you*, *will you*, and *would you*.**

EXAMPLES Call the doctor for me.
Would you call the doctor for me?

Give me a cup of coffee.
Could you give me a cup of coffee, please?

1. Repeat the sentence.
2. Give me your paper.
3. Spell your name.
4. Tell me your phone number.

EXERCISE 29 **Make these sentences more polite by using *would like*.**

EXAMPLE Do you want some help?
Would you like some help?

1. I want to ask you a question.
2. The teacher wants to speak with you.
3. Do you want to try out the oven?
4. Yes. I want to see if it works.

EXERCISE 30 **Make each suggestion more polite by putting it in the form of a negative question.**

EXAMPLES Plug it in.
Why don't you plug it in?

Let's eat now.
Why don't we eat now?

1. Take a sweater.
2. Let's turn off the light.
3. Turn left here.
4. Let's leave early.

EXERCISE 31 **ABOUT YOU** **Make a statement of preference using *would rather*.**

EXAMPLE own a house / a condominium
I'd rather own a condominium than a house.

1. live in the U.S. / in another country
2. own a condominium / rent an apartment
3. have young neighbors / old neighbors
4. have wood floors / carpeted floors
5. live in the center of the city / in a suburb
6. drive to work / take public transportation
7. pay my rent by check / with cash
8. have nosy neighbors / noisy neighbors

EXERCISE 32   **ABOUT YOU**   Ask a question of preference with the words given. Another student will answer.

EXAMPLE   eat Chinese food / Italian food

A: Would you rather eat Chinese food or Italian food?
B: I'd rather eat Italian food.

1. read fact / fiction
2. watch funny movies / serious movies
3. listen to classical music / popular music
4. visit Europe / Africa
5. own a large luxury car / a small sports car
6. watch a soccer game / take part in a soccer game
7. write a letter / receive a letter
8. cook / eat in a restaurant

EXERCISE 33   This is a conversation between a seller (S) and a buyer (B) at a garage sale. Make this conversation more polite by using modals and other polite expressions in place of the underlined words. Answers may vary.

CD 3, TR 11

        May I help you?
S: ~~What do you want?~~
          (example)

B: I'm interested in that lamp. <u>Show it to me</u>. Does it work?
                                 (1)

S: I'll go and get a light bulb. <u>Wait a minute</u>.
                                      (2)

(*A few minutes later*)

B: <u>Plug it in</u>.
   (3)

S: You see? It works fine.

B: How much do you want for it?

S: This is one of a pair. I have another one just like it. They're $10 each.

    <u>I prefer to sell</u> them together.
        (4)

B: <u>Give them both to me for $15</u>.
             (5)

S: I'll have to ask my husband.

    (*A few seconds later*)

    My husband says he'll sell them to you for $17.

B: Fine. I'll take them. Will you take a check?

S: <u>I prefer to</u> have cash.
      (6)

B: I only have five dollars on me.

S: OK. I'll take a check. <u>Show me some identification</u>.
(7)

B: Here's my driver's license.

S: That's fine. Just write the check to James Kucinski.

B: <u>Spell your name for me</u>.
(8)

S: K-U-C-I-N-S-K-I.

Summary of Lesson 8

Modals

MODAL	EXAMPLE	EXPLANATION
can	I **can** stay in this apartment until March. I **can** carry my bicycle up to my apartment. You **can't** paint the walls without the landlord's permission. **Can** I borrow your pen? **Can** you turn off the light, please?	Permission Ability/Possibility Prohibition Asking permission Request
should	You **should** be friendly with your neighbors. You **shouldn't** leave the air conditioner on. It wastes electricity.	A good idea A bad idea
may	**May** I borrow your pen? You **may** leave the room. You **may not** talk during a test. I **may** move next month. The landlord **may** have an extra key.	Asking permission Giving permission Prohibition Future possibility Present possibility
might	I **might** move next month. The landlord **might** have an extra key.	Future possibility Present possibility
must	The landlord **must** install smoke detectors. You **must not** change the locks. Mary has a cat carrier. She **must** have a cat.	Rule or law: Official tone Prohibition: Official tone Conclusion/Deduction
would	**Would** you help me move?	Request
would like	I **would like** to use your phone.	Want
would rather	I **would rather** live in Florida than in Maine.	Preference
could	In my country, I **couldn't** choose my own apartment. The government gave me one. In my country, I **could** attend college for free. **Could** you help me move? **Could** I borrow your car?	Past permission Past ability Request Asking permission

Related Expressions

EXPRESSION	EXAMPLE	EXPLANATION
have to	She **has to** leave. He **had to** leave work early today.	Necessity Past necessity
have got to	She **has got to** see a doctor. I**'ve got to** move.	Necessity
not have to	You **don't have to** pay your rent with cash. You can pay by check.	No necessity
had better	You **had better** pay your rent on time, or the landlord will ask you to leave. You**'d better** get permission before changing the locks.	Warning
be supposed to	We**'re not supposed to** have a dog here. I **was supposed to** pay my rent by the fifth of the month, but I forgot.	Reporting a rule or obligation
be able to	The teacher **is able to** use modals correctly.	Ability
be permitted to be allowed to	We**'re not permitted to** park here overnight. We**'re not allowed to** park here overnight.	Permission

Editing Advice

1. After a modal, use the base form.

   I must ~~to~~ study.

   I can help~~ing~~ you now.

2. A modal has no ending.

   He can~~s~~ cook.

3. Don't put two modals together. Change the second modal to another form.

   She will ~~must~~ *have to* take the test.

4. Don't forget *to* after *be permitted, be allowed, be supposed,* and *be able.*

   We're not permitted *to* talk during a test.

5. Don't forget *be* before *permitted to, allowed to, supposed to,* and *able to.*

    am

    I ^ not supposed to pay my rent late.

6. Use the correct word order in a question.

    should I

    What ~~I should~~ do about my problem?

7. Don't use *can* for past. Use *could* + a base form.

    couldn't go

    I ~~can't went~~ to the party last week.

8. Don't forget *would* before *rather.*

    'd

    I ^ rather live in Canada than in the U.S.

9. Don't forget *had* before *better.*

    'd

    You ^ better take a sweater. It's going to get cold.

10. Don't forget *have* before *got to.*

    've

    It's late. I ^ got to go.

11. Don't use *maybe* before a verb.

    may

    It ~~maybe will~~ rain later.

Editing Quiz

Some of the shaded words and phrases have mistakes. Find the mistakes and correct them. If the shaded words are correct, write C.

    've

A: I ^ got to move when my lease is up.
    (example)   C

B: Why do you have to move? You have a great apartment.
    (example)

A: I want to get a dog, but we not permitted to have dogs in my building.
    (1)

B: Maybe your landlord won't find out.

A: Of course he'll find out. I will have to take the dog out for a walk a
    (2)

few times a day.

B: How will he know? My landlord only comes once a month on the day
    (3)

we supposed to pay the rent.
    (4)

A: My landlord lives on the first floor.

B: Oh. That's a problem. What about a cat? Cats are allow in your
                                                              (5)
building, right? He maybe will let you have a cat.
                     (6)

A: Cats are permit, but I can't be around cats.
                (7)   (8)

B: Why you can't be around cats?
          (9)

A: I'm allergic to them. Anyway, I rather have a dog. Dogs are better
                                    (10)
companions.

B: If you want a companion, maybe you should find a roommate.
                                         (11)

A: I used to have a roommate, but we can't agreed on a lot of things.
                                          (12)
So when he moved out, I decided that I better not to have another
                                      (13)   (14)
roommate.

Lesson 8 Test/Review

PART 1 This is a conversation between two friends. Circle the correct
expression in parentheses ( ) to complete the conversation.

A: I'm moving on Saturday. (Could / May) you help me?
                                 (example)

B: I (should / would) like to help you, but I have a bad back. I went to
          (1)
my doctor last week, and she told me that I (shouldn't / don't have to)
                                                  (2)
lift anything heavy for a while. (Can / Would) I help you any other
                                       (3)
way besides moving?

A: Yes. I don't have enough boxes. (Should / Would) you help me find
                                              (4)
some?

B: Sure. I (have to / must) go shopping this afternoon. I'll pick up some
               (5)
boxes while I'm at the supermarket.

A: Boxes can be heavy. You (would / had) better not lift them yourself.
                                    (6)

B: Don't worry. I'll have someone put them in my car for me.

A: Thanks. I don't have a free minute. I (couldn't go / can't went) to
                                                  (7)
class all last week. There's so much to do.

B: I know what you mean. You (*might / must*) be tired.
(8)

A: I am. I have another favor to ask. (*Can / Would*) I borrow your van
(9)

on Saturday?

B: I (*should / have to*) work on Saturday. How about Sunday? I
(10)

(*must not / don't have to*) work on Sunday.
(11)

A: That's impossible. I (*'ve got to / should*) move out on Saturday. The
(12)

new tenants are moving in Sunday morning.

B: Let me ask my brother. He has a van too. He (*must / might*) be able
(13)

to let you use his van. He (*has to / should*) work Saturday too, but
(14)

only for half a day.

A: Thanks. I'd appreciate it if you could ask him.

B: Why are you moving? You have a great apartment.

A: We decided to move to the suburbs. It's quieter there. And I want to

have a dog. I (*shouldn't / 'm not supposed to*) have a dog in my
(15)

present apartment. But my new landlord says I (*might / may*) have
(16)

a dog.

B: I (*had / would*) rather have a cat. They're easier to take care of.
(17)

PART 2 **Fill in the blanks to complete the sentences. In some cases, more
than one answer is possible.**

1. I don't like my apartment. I have such noisy neighbors. I ___*can*___
   (example)
   hear their music all the time. Sometimes I _____ study or sleep
   at night because it's so loud. I don't know why they play the music so
   loud. They _____ be deaf!

2. I take my bike upstairs because we're not _____ to leave our bikes
   in the hallway.

3. Stop! Put down that hammer. You'd _____ not make a hole
   in the wall to put up that picture, or the landlord will get angry. He
   _____ even keep your security deposit.

4. I'd _____ take public transportation _____ go to work
   by car. That's why I moved close to the train.

5. Your brother lives alone. He _____ be lonely. Maybe he _____ get a roommate.

6. My lease says, "Tenants _____ not have a water bed."

7. My landlady is raising my rent. I've _____ to find a new apartment.

8. My mother's coming to visit, so I _____ to clean my apartment.

9. I can help you move on Saturday because I don't _____ to work that day.

10. Do you see that sign? It says "No Parking in Front of Building." You're not _____ to park here. Park in the back.

Expansion

Classroom Activities

① **A student will read one of the following problems out loud to the class, pretending that this is his or her problem. Other students will ask for more information and give advice about this problem.**

EXAMPLE   My mother-in-law comes to visit all the time. When she's here, she always criticizes everything we do. I told my wife that I don't want her here, but she says, "It's my mother, and I want her here." What should I do?

A: How long does she usually stay?

B: She might stay for about two weeks or longer.

C: How does she criticize you? What does she say?

B: She says I should help my wife more.

D: Well, I agree with her. You should help with housework. What other problems are you having with her?

B: My children aren't allowed to watch TV after 8.00 P.M. But my mother-in-law lets them watch TV as long as they want.

E: You'd better have a talk with her and tell her your rules.

Problem 1.   My mother is 80 years old, and she lives with us. It's very hard on my family to take care of her. We'd like to put her in a nursing home, where she can get better care. Mother refuses to go. What can we do?

Problem 2. I'm sixteen years old. I want to get a part-time job after school. I want to save money to buy a car. My parents say I won't have enough time to study. But I think I can do both. How can I convince my parents?

Problem 3. I have a nice one-bedroom apartment with a beautiful view of a park and a lake. I live with my wife and one child. My friends from out of town often come to visit and want to stay at my apartment. In the last year, ten people came to visit us. I like to have visitors, but sometimes they stay for weeks. It's hard on my family with such a small apartment. What should I tell my friends when they want to visit?

Problem 4. My upstairs neighbors make noise all the time. I can't sleep at night. I have asked them three times to be quieter, and each time they said they would. But the noise still continues. What should I do?

Problem 5. My roommate brings friends home all the time. They eat pizza, drink sodas, and watch TV. When they leave, the apartment is a mess. What should I do?

❷ Work with a partner from your own country, if possible. Talk about some laws in your country that are different from laws in the U.S. Present this information to the class.

EXAMPLE   Citizens must vote in my country. In the U.S., they don't have to vote.

People are supposed to carry identification papers at all times. In the U.S., people don't have to carry identification papers.

Talk
About It

❶ Compare renting an apartment here with renting an apartment in another country or city.

❷ How did you find your present apartment?

❸ What are some of the things you like about the place where you live? What are some of the things you dislike?

Write

About It

1 Write a short composition comparing rules in an apartment in this city with rules in an apartment in your hometown or native country.

2 Find out what a student has to do to register for the first time at this school. You may want to visit the registrar's office to interview a worker there. Write a short composition explaining to a new student the steps for admission and registration.

3 Write about the differences between rules at this school and rules at another school you attended. Are students allowed to do things here that they can't do in another school?

Comparing School Rules

The rules and customs at this school, Harper College,
and my college back home in the Philippines are different. At
this school, we don't have to call our teachers "Mr." or "Ms."
We can call them by their first names. In the Philippines,
students must call teachers by their title, "Professor"...

 For more practice using grammar in context, please visit our Web site.

Grammar
The Present Perfect

The Present Perfect Continuous[1]

Context
The Internet

[1]The *present perfect continuous* is sometimes called the *present perfect progressive*.

9.1 The Present Perfect Tense—An Overview

We form the present perfect with *have* or *has* + the past participle.

Subject	*have*	Past Participle	Complement	Explanation
I	have	been	in the U.S. for three years.	Use *have* with I, *you*, *we*, *they*, and plural nouns.
You	have	used	your computer a lot.	
We	have	written	a job résumé.	
They	have	bought	a new computer.	
Computers	have	changed	the world.	

Subject	*has*	Past Participle	Complement	Explanation
My sister	has	gotten	her degree.	Use *has* with *he*, *she*, *it*, and singular nouns.
She	has	found	a job as a programmer.	
My father	has	helped	me.	
The computer	has	changed	a lot over the years.	

There	*has/have*	*been*	Complement	Explanation
There	has *sing*	been	a problem with my computer.	After *there*, we use *has* or *have*, depending on the noun that follows. Use *has* with a singular noun. Use *have* with a plural noun.
There	have *plural*	been	many changes with personal computers.	

Google

Before You Read

1. Do you use the Internet a lot? Why?

2. What search engine do you usually use?

CD 3, TR 12

Read the following Web article. Pay special attention to the present perfect tense.

Since its start in 1998, Google **has become** one of the most popular search engines. It **has grown** from a research project in the dormitory room of two college students to a business that now employs approximately 20,000 people.

Larry Page and Sergey Brin

Google's founders, Larry Page and Sergey Brin, met in 1995 when they were in their twenties and graduate students in computer science at Stanford University in California. They realized that Internet search was a very important field and began working together to make searching easier. Both Page and Brin left their studies at Stanford to work on their project. Interestingly, they **have** never **returned** to finish their degrees.

Brin was born in Russia, but he **has lived** in the U.S. since he was five years old. His father was a mathematician in Russia. Page, whose parents were computer experts, **has been** interested in computers since he was six years old.

When Google started in 1998, it did 10,000 searches a day. Today it does 235 million searches a day in 40 languages. It indexes[2] 1 trillion Web pages.

How is Google different from other search engines? **Have** you ever **noticed** how many ads and banners there are on other search engines? News, sports scores, stock prices, links for shopping, mortgage rates, and more fill other search engines. Brin and Page wanted a clean home page. They believed that people come to the Internet to search for specific information, not to be hit with a lot of unwanted data. The success of Google over its rivals[3] **has proved** that this is true.

Over the years, Google **has added** new features to its Web site: Google Images, where you can type in a word and get thousands of pictures; Google News, which takes you to today's news; Google Maps; and more. But one thing **hasn't changed:** the clean opening page that Google offers its users.

In 2009, Forbes.com listed Page and Brin as having net worths of $12 billion each, at 36 and 35 years old.

[2]*To index* means to sort, organize, and categorize information.
[3]*Rivals* are competitors.

The Present Perfect; The Present Perfect Continuous **281**

EXERCISE 1 Underline the present perfect tense in each sentence. Then tell if the sentence is true or false.

EXAMPLE Google __has become__ a very popular search engine. T

1. Google has grown over the years.
2. Sergey Brin has lived in the U.S. all his life. F
3. Larry Page and Sergey Brin have known each other since they were children.
4. Larry Page has been interested in computers since he was a child.
5. Brin and Page have returned to college to finish their degrees.
6. Brin and Page have become rich.
7. The noun "Google" has become a verb.

9.2 The Past Participle

The past participle of regular verbs ends in -ed. The past participle is the same as the past form for regular verbs.

FORMS			EXAMPLES
Base Form	**Past Form**	**Past Participle**	I **work** every day. I **worked** yesterday. I **have worked** all week.
work improve	worked improved	worked improved	

The past participle of many irregular verbs is the same as the past form.

FORMS			EXAMPLES
Base Form	**Past Form**	**Past Participle**	We **have** a new car now. We **had** an old car, but we sold it. We **have had** our new car for two months.
have buy	had bought	had bought	

The past participle of some irregular verbs is different from the past form.

FORMS			EXAMPLES
Base Form	**Past Form**	**Past Participle**	I **write** a composition once a week. I **wrote** a composition yesterday. I **have written** five compositions this semester.
go write	went wrote	gone written	

For the following verbs, the base form, past form, and past participle are all different.

Base Form	Past Form	Past Participle
become	became	become
come	came	come
run	ran	run
blow	blew	blown
draw	drew	drawn
fly	flew	flown
grow	grew	grown
know	knew	known
throw	threw	thrown
swear	swore	sworn
tear	tore	torn
wear	wore	worn
break	broke	broken
choose	chose	chosen
freeze	froze	frozen
speak	spoke	spoken
steal *robar*	stole	stolen
begin	began	begun
drink	drank	drunk
ring	rang	rung
sing	sang	sung
sink *hundir*	sank	sunk
swim	swam	swum

Base Form	Past Form	Past Participle
arise *levantarse*	arose	arisen
bite *morder*	bit	bitten
drive	drove	driven
ride	rode	ridden
rise *subir*	rose	risen
write	wrote	written
be	was/were	been
eat	ate	eaten
fall	fell	fallen
forgive	forgave	forgiven
give	gave	given
mistake	mistook	mistaken
see	saw	seen
shake	shook	shaken
take	took	taken
do	did	done
forget	forgot	forgotten
get	got	gotten
go	went	gone
lie	lay	lain
prove	proved	proven (or proved)
show	showed	shown (or showed)

grow up.

EXERCISE 2   **Write the past participle of these verbs.**

EXAMPLE   eat ___eaten___

1. go _gone_
2. see _seen_
3. look _looken_
4. study _studi_
5. bring _bringen_
6. take _taken_
7. say _said_
8. be _been_
9. find _found_
10. leave _left_

11. live _lived_
12. know _known_
13. like _lik_
14. fall _fallen_
15. feel _feelen_
16. come _comes_
17. break _broken_
18. wear _worm_
19. choose _choosen_
20. drive _driven_

21. write _written_
22. put _put_
23. begin _begun_
24. want _wanted_
25. get _gotten/got_
26. fly _flown_
27. sit _sat_
28. drink _drunk_
29. grow _grown_
30. give _given_

9.3 The Present Perfect—Contractions and Negatives

EXAMPLES	EXPLANATION
I've had a lot of experience with computers. **We've** read the story about Google. **He's** been interested in computers since he was a child. **There's** been an increase in searching over the years.	We can make a contraction with subject pronouns and *have* or *has*. I have = I've He has = He's You have = You've She has = She's We have = We've It has = It's They have = They've There has = There's
Larry's lived in the U.S. all his life. **Sergey's** been in the U.S. since he was five years old.	Most singular nouns can contract with *has*.
I **haven't** studied programming. Brin **hasn't** returned to college.	Negative contractions: *have not = haven't* *has not = hasn't*

Language Note: The **'s** in *he's*, *she's*, *it's*, and *there's* can mean *has* or *is*. The word following the contraction will tell you what the contraction means.
     He**'s** working. = He *is* working.
     He**'s** worked. = He *has* worked.

EXERCISE **3**   **Fill in the blanks to form the present perfect. Make a contraction if possible.**

EXAMPLE   You <u>'ve</u>_____ bought a new computer.

1. I _____ learned a lot about computers.
2. We _____ read the story about Google.
3. Larry _____ known Sergey since they were at Stanford University.
4. They (not) _____ known each other since they were children.
5. It _____ been easy for me to learn about computers.
6. You _____ used the Internet many times.
7. Larry and Sergey (not) _____ finished their degrees.

9.4 Adding an Adverb

Subject	has/ have	Adverb	Past Participle	Complement	Explanation
Page and Brin	**have**	never	**finished**	their degrees.	You can put an adverb between the auxiliary verb (*have/has*) and the past participle.
They	**have**	already*	**made**	a lot of money.	
They	**have**	even	**become**	billionaires.	
Larry Page	**has**	always	**been**	interested in computers.	
You	**have**	probably	**used**	a search engine.	

Language Note: *Already* frequently comes at the end of the verb phrase.
They have made a lot of money **already**.

EXERCISE 4 Add the word in parentheses ( ) to the sentence.

EXAMPLE   You have gotten an e-mail account. (probably)
<u>**You have probably gotten an e-mail account.**</u>

1. The teacher has given a test on Lesson 8. (already)
   _____

2. We have heard of Page and Brin. (never)
   _____

3. They have been interested in search technology. (always)
   _____

4. You have used Google. (probably)
   _____

5. Brin hasn't finished his degree. (even)
   _____

6. Brin and Page have become billionaires. (already)
   _____

9.5 The Present Perfect—Statements and Questions

Compare affirmative statements and questions.

Wh-Word	have/has	Subject	have/has	Past Participle	Complement	Short Answer
		Larry	**has**	**lived**	in the U.S. all his life.	
	Has	Sergey		**lived**	in the U.S. all his life?	No, he **hasn't**.
How long	**has**	Sergey		**lived**	in the U.S.?	Since 1979.

Language Note: For a short *yes* answer, we cannot make a contraction.
Has Larry lived in the U.S. all his life? Yes, he has. (Not: *he's*)

Compare negative statements and questions.

Wh-Word	haven't/hasn't	Subject	haven't/hasn't	Past Participle	Complement
		They	**haven't**	**finished**	their degrees.
Why	**haven't**	they		**finished**	their degrees?

EXERCISE 5 Change the statement to a question, using the word(s) in parentheses.

EXAMPLE Google has changed the way people search. (how)
<u>How has *Google changed the way people search?*</u>

1. I have used several search engines. (which ones)

_____

2. Larry and Sergey haven't finished their degrees. (why)

_____

3. They have made a lot of money. (how much)

_____

4. Sergey has been in the U.S. for many years. (how long)

_____

5. Larry and Sergey have hired many people to work for Google.
(how many)

_____

6. We have used the computer lab several times this semester. (how
many times)

_____

7. The memory and speed of computers have increased. (why)

_____

8. Computers have become part of our daily lives. (how)

_____

9.6 Continuation from Past to Present

We use the present perfect tense to show that an action or state started in the past and continues to the present.

Past ◄——————————————————————— Now - ► Future

┌─────────────────────────────┐
│ I **have had** my computer   │
│ **for two months.**   │
└─────────────────────────────┘

EXAMPLES	EXPLANATION
Larry Page **has been** interested in computers **for many years.** My sister **has been** a programmer **for three years.**	Use _for_ + an amount of time: _for two months, for three years, for one hour, for a long time,_ etc.
Brin's family **has been** in the U.S. **since 1979.** I **have had** my computer **since March.** Personal computers **have been** popular **since the 1980s.**	Use _since_ with the date, month, year, etc., that the action began.
Brin **has been** interested in computers since he **was** a child. I **have had** an e-mail account since I **bought** my computer.	Use _since_ with the beginning of the continuous action or state. The verb in the _since_ clause is simple past.
How long has Brin's family been in the U.S.? **How long** have you had your computer?	Use _how long_ to ask about the amount of time from the past to the present.
Larry Page has **always** lived in the U.S. He has **always** been interested in computers.	We use the present perfect with _always_ to show that an action began in the past and continues to the present.
My grandmother has **never** used a computer. Google has **never** put advertising on its opening page.	We use the present perfect with _never_ to show that something has not occurred from the past to the present.

EXERCISE 6   **Fill in the blanks with the missing words.**

EXAMPLE   I've known my best friend ___since___ we were in high school.

1. My brother has been in the U.S. _____ 1998.

2. My mother _____ never been in the U.S.

3. How _____ have you been in the U.S.?

4. I've known the teacher since I _____ to study at this school.

5. My sister's _____ married for two years.

6. She's had the same job _____ ten years.

7. My best friend and I _____ known each other since we _____ in elementary school.

8. She' _____ been a student at this school _____ September.

9. I've had my car for three years. _____ long have you _____ your car?

10. I'm interested in computers. I' _____ _____ interested in computers since I was in high school.

11. _____ always wanted to have my own business.

EXERCISE 7   **ABOUT YOU** **Write true statements using the present perfect with the words given and *for, since, always,* or *never*. Share your sentences with the class.**

EXAMPLES   know ___My parents have known each other for over 40 years.___

have ___I've had my cell phone since March.___

want ___I've always wanted to learn English.___

1. have _____

2. be _____

3. want _____

4. know _____

EXERCISE 8   **ABOUT YOU** **Make statements with *always*.**

EXAMPLE   Name something you've always thought about.
I've always thought about my future.

1. Name something you've always enjoyed.

2. Name a person you've always liked. _I've always liked Messi_

3. Name something you've always wanted to do. *I have always wanted a car*

4. Name something you've always wanted to have. *- I have*

5. Name something you've always been interested in.

EXERCISE 9 **ABOUT YOU** Make statements with *never*.

EXAMPLE Name a machine you've never used.
I've never used a fax machine.

1. Name a movie you've never seen.

2. Name a food you've never liked.

3. Name a subject you've never studied.

4. Name a city you've never visited.

5. Name a sport you've never played.

6. Name a food you've never tasted.

EXERCISE 10 **ABOUT YOU** Write four sentences telling about things you've always done (or been). Share your sentences with the class.

EXAMPLES I've always cooked the meals in my family.

I've always been lazy. *perezoso.*
p.prof.

1. *I've always played volleyball   I've always been upsetting (moleste*

2. *I've always cooked Peruvian food.*

3. *I've always been upsetting*

4. *I've always been happy*

EXERCISE 11 **ABOUT YOU** Write four sentences telling about things you've never done (or been) but would like to. Share your sentences with the class.

EXAMPLES I've never studied photography, but I'd like to.

I've never acted in a play, but I'd like to.

1. _____

2. _____

3. _____

4. _____

9.7 The Simple Present vs. the Present Perfect

EXAMPLES	EXPLANATION
a. Larry Page **is** in California. b. Larry Page **has been** in California since he was in his twenties. a. He **loves** computers. b. He **has** always **loved** computers. a. Google **doesn't have** advertising on its home page. b. Google **has** never **had** advertising on its home page. a. **Do** you **work** at a computer company? Yes, I **do**. b. **Have** you always **worked** at a computer company? Yes, I **have**.	Sentences (a) refer only to the present. Sentences (b) connect the past to the present.

EXERCISE 12 Read each statement about your teacher. Then ask the teacher a question beginning with the words given. Include *always* in your question. Your teacher will answer.

EXAMPLE   You're a teacher. Have you _____ *always been a teacher* _____?

No. I was an accountant before I became a teacher. I've only been a teacher for five years.

1. You teach English. Have you _____
_____?

2. You work at this college/school. Have you _____
_____?

3. You think about grammar. Have you _____
_____?

4. English is easy for you. Has English _____
_____?

5. Your last name is _____. Has your last name
_____?

6. You're interested in languages. Have you _____
_____?

7. You live in this city. Have you _____
_____?

EXERCISE **Fill in the blanks with the missing words.**

CD 3, TR 13

Two students meet by chance in the computer lab.

A: ____**Have**____ you ____**been**____ in the U.S. for long?
  (example)   *(example)*

B: No, I _____.
        (1)

A: How _____ _____ you been in the U.S.?
         (2)   *(3)*

B: I _____ _____ here for about a year.
       (4)   *(5)*

A: Where do you come from?

B: Burundi.

A: Burundi? I _____ never _____ of it. Where is it?
              (6)   *(7)*

B: It's a small country in Central Africa.

A: Do you have a map? Can you show me where it is?

B: Let's go on the Internet. We can do a search.

A: Did you learn to use a computer in your country?

B: No. When I came here, a volunteer at my church gave me her old computer. Before, I didn't know anything about computers. I've _____ a lot about computers since I came here.
       (8)

A: Oh, now I see Burundi. It's very small. It's near Congo.

B: Yes, it is.

A: Why did you come to the U.S.?

B: My country _____ political problems for many years.
                  (9)
It wasn't safe to live there. My family left in 1995.

A: So you _____ _____ here since 1995?
             (10)   *(11)*

B: No. First we lived in a refugee camp in Zambia.

A: I _____ never _____ of Zambia either.
       (12)   *(13)*
Can we search for it on the Internet?

B: Here it is.

A: You speak English very well. Is English the language of Burundi?

B: No. Kirundi is the official language. Also French. I _____
                                                        (14)
_____ French since I was a small child. Where are you from?
(15)
(continued)

The Present Perfect; The Present Perfect Continuous   **291**

A: I'm from North Dakota.

B: I _____ never _____ of North Dakota. Is it in the U.S.?
(16)   (17)

A: Yes, it is. Let's search for an American map on the Internet. Here it is.

Winter in North Dakota is very cold. It's cold here too.

B: I don't know how people live in a cold climate. I _____
(18)

never _____ in a cold climate before. I _____
(19)   (20)

always _____ near the Equator.
(21)

A: Don't worry. You'll be OK. You just need warm clothes for the winter.

B: I have class now. I've got to go.

A: I _____ _____ so much about your country in such a
(22)   (23)

short time.

B: It's easy to learn things fast using a computer and a search engine.

9.8 The Present Perfect vs. the Simple Past

Do not confuse the present perfect with the simple past.

EXAMPLES	EXPLANATION
Compare: a. Sergey Brin **came** to the U.S. in 1979. b. Sergey Brin **has been** in the U.S. since 1979. a. Brin and Page **started** Google in 1998. b. Google **has been** popular since 1998.	Sentences (a) show a single action in the past. This action does not continue. Sentences (b) show the continuation of an action or state from the past to the present.
a. When **did** Brin **come** to the U.S.? b. How long **has** Brin **been** in the U.S.?	Question (a) with *when* uses the simple past tense. Question (b) with *how long* uses the present perfect tense.

EXERCISE 14 Fill in the blanks with the simple past or the present perfect of the verb in parentheses ( ).

CD 3, TR 14

A: Do you like to surf the Internet?

B: Of course, I do. I 've had _____ my Internet connection since 1999,
(example: have)

and I love it. A couple of months ago, I _____ a new computer
(1 buy)

with lots of memory and speed. And last month I _____
(2 change)

to a better service provider. Now I can surf much faster.

A: What kind of things do you search for?

B: Lots of things. I _____ to learn about the stock market, and with
(3 always/want)
the Web, I can start to learn. Last week I _____ my first investment
(4 make)
in the stock market.

A: Do you ever buy products online?

B: Sometimes I do. Last month, I _____ a great Web site where
(5 find)
I can download music for 99¢. So far
I _____ about a hundred songs,
(6 download)
and I _____ several CDs. My old
(7 make)
computer _____ a CD burner,
(8 not/have)
so I'm very happy with my new one.

A: _____ your old computer?
(9 you/sell)

B: No. It was about eight years old. I just _____ the hard drive
(10 remove)
and _____ the computer on top of the garbage dumpster.
(11 leave)
When I _____ by a few hours later, it was gone.
(12 pass)
Someone _____ it.
(13 take)

A: Was your new computer expensive?

B: Yes, but I _____ a great deal online.
(14 get)

A: I _____ my computer for three years, and it seems so old by
(15 have)
comparison to today's computers. But it's too expensive to buy a new
one every year.

B: There's a joke about computers: "When is a computer old?"

A: I don't know. When?

B: As soon as you get it out of the box!

We use the present perfect continuous for a continuous action that started in the past and continues to the present.

EXAMPLES	EXPLANATION
I **have been using** the Internet since 9 A.M. I **have been surfing** the Web for 2 hours. We **have been learning** a lot about computers.	A continuous action started in the past and continues to the present.

Genealogy

Before
You Read

1. Do you think it's important to know your family's history? Why or why not?

2. What would you like to know about your ancestors?

CD 3, TR 15

Read the following magazine article. Pay special attention to the present perfect and the present perfect continuous tenses.

In the last 30 years, genealogy **has become** one of America's most popular hobbies. If you type *genealogy* in a search engine, you can find about 90 million hits. If you type *family history*, you will get about 50 million hits. The percentage of the U.S. population interested in family history **has been increasing** steadily. This increase probably has to do with the ease of searching on the Internet.

The number of genealogy Web sites **has been growing** accordingly as people ask themselves: Where does my family come from? How long **has** my family **been** in the U.S.? Why did they come here? How did they come here? What kind of people were they?

Genealogy is a lifelong hobby for many. The average family historian **has been doing** genealogy for 14 years, according to a 2001 study. Most family historians are over 40. Cyndi Howells, from Washington State, quit her job in 1992 and **has been working** on her family history ever since. She **has created** a Web site called Cyndi's List to help others with their search. Her Web site has over 260,000 resources. Since its start in 1992, her Web site **has had** millions of visitors. Every day it gets about 15,000 visitors. Over the years, she **has added** many new links and **deleted** old ones.

Although the Internet **has made** research easier for amateur genealogists, it is only the beginning for serious family historians. Researchers still need to go to courthouses and libraries to find public records, such as land deeds,[4] obituaries,[5] wedding notices, and tax records. Another good source of information is the U.S. Census. Early census records are not complete, but since the mid-1800s, the U.S. Census **has been keeping** detailed records of family members, their ages, occupations, and places of birth.

Are you interested in knowing more about your ancestors and their stories, their country or countries, and how you fit into the history of your family? Maybe genealogy is a good hobby for you.

9.10 The Present Perfect Continuous—Forms

Subject	have/has	been	Present Participle	Complement
I	have	been	using	the Internet for two hours.
We	have	been	reading	about search engines.
You	have	been	studying	computers.
They	have	been	living	in California.
He	has	been	writing	since 1:00 P.M.
She	has	been	surfing	the Internet all day.
It	has	been	raining	all day.

Language Note: To form the negative, put *not* between *have* or *has* and *been*.
   You **have *not* been** listening.
   She **has*n't* been** working hard.

[4]A *land deed* is a document that shows who the owner of the land is.
[5]*Obituaries* are death notices posted in the newspaper.

(continued)

Compare affirmative statements and questions.

Wh-Word	have/has	Subject	have/has	been + Verb -ing	Complement	Short Answer
		Cyndi	has	been working	on her family history.	
	Has	she		been working	on her Web site?	Yes, she has.
How long	has	she		been working	on her Web site?	Since 1992.

Compare negative statements and questions.

Wh-Word	haven't/hasn't	Subject	haven't/hasn't	been + Verb -ing	Complement
		They	haven't	been using	the public library.
Why	haven't	they		been using	the public library?

EXERCISE 15 **Fill in the blanks with the present perfect continuous form of the verb in parentheses ( ).**

EXAMPLE How long _____has_____ Cyndi ___been managing___ a
                                                    (example: manage)
genealogy Web site?

1. Interest in genealogy _____.
                                     (grow)

2. Cyndi _____ on her family history since 1992.
                  (work)

3. Cyndi _____ all over the U.S. to genealogy groups.
                  (lecture)

4. The number of genealogy Web sites _____.
                                                (increase)

5. How long _____ the U.S. Census

   _____ records?
        (keep)

6. _____ you _____ on a family tree for
                                          (work)

   your family?

7. People _____ the Internet to do family research
                  (use)

   since the 1990s.

8. My family _____ in the U.S. for many generations.
                  (not/live)

9.11 The Present Perfect Continuous—Use

We use the present perfect continuous tense to show that an action or state started in the past and continues to the present.

Past ◄─────────┌─────────────────────────┐ Now - - - - - - - - - - - - - - - - - - ► Future
│ He **has been living** in │
│ the U.S. since 1979. │
└─────────────────────────┘

EXAMPLES	EXPLANATION
Cyndi **has been working** on her family tree since 1992. Sergey Brin **has been living** in the U.S. for more than 30 years.	We use *for* and *since* to show the time spent on an activity from past to present.
He **has been living** in the U.S. since 1979. OR He **has lived** in the U.S. since 1979.	With some verbs (*live, work, study, teach,* and *wear*), we can use either the present perfect or the present perfect continuous with actions that began in the past and continue to the present. The meaning is the same.
My father *is working* on the family tree right now. He **has been working** on it since 9 A.M.	If the action is still happening, use the present perfect continuous, not the present perfect.
Google **has become** one of the most popular search engines. I **have had** my computer for three months.	We do not use the continuous form with nonaction verbs. See below for a list of nonaction verbs.
I **have** always **loved** computers. My grandmother **has** never **used** a computer.	Do not use the continuous form with *always* and *never*.
Action: I **have been thinking** *about* doing a family tree. **Nonaction:** I **have** always **thought** *that* genealogy is an interesting hobby.	*Think* can be an action or nonaction verb, depending on its meaning. 　　*Think about* = action verb 　　*Think that* = nonaction verb
Nonaction: Some people **have had** a lot of success in locating information. **Action:** We **have been having** a hard time locating information about our ancestors.	*Have* is usually a nonaction verb. However, *have* is an action verb in these expressions: *have experience, have a hard time, have a good time, have difficulty,* and *have trouble.*

Nonaction verbs:

like	know	see
love	believe	seem
hate	think (that)	cost
want	care (about)	own
need	understand	become
prefer	remember	have (for possession)

EXERCISE 16 **ABOUT YOU** Write true statements using the present perfect continuous with the words given and *for* or *since*. Share your sentences with the class.

EXAMPLE   work _My brother has been working as a waiter for six years._

1. study English _____

2. work _____

3. live _____

4. use _____

5. study _____

EXERCISE 17 **ABOUT YOU** Read aloud each of the following present tense questions. Another student will answer. If the answer is *yes*, add a present perfect continuous question with *"How long have you . . . ?"*

EXAMPLE   Do you play a musical instrument?

A: Do you play a musical instrument?
B: Yes. I play the piano.
A: How long have you been playing the piano?
B: I've been playing the piano since I was a child.

1. Do you drive?

2. Do you work?

3. Do you use the Internet?

4. Do you wear glasses?

5. Do you play a musical instrument?

EXERCISE 18 Ask the teacher questions with *"How long . . . ?"* and the present perfect continuous form of the verb given. The teacher will answer your questions.

EXAMPLE   speak English

A: How long have you been speaking English?
B: I've been speaking English all[6] my life.

1. teach English

2. work at this school

3. live in this city

4. use this book

5. live at your present address

---

[6]We do not use the preposition *for* before *all*.

EXERCISE 19   **Fill in the blanks in the following conversations. Answers may vary.**

EXAMPLE   **A:** Do you wear glasses?

     B: Yes, I _____do_____.

     A: How long ___have___ you ___been wearing___ glasses?

     B: I _'ve been wearing_ glasses since I ___was___ in high school.

1. A: Are you working on your family history?

     B: Yes, I am.

     A: How long _____ you _____ on your

     family history?

     B: I _____ on it for about ten years.

2. A: Is your sister surfing the Internet?

     B: Yes, she _____.

     A: How long _____ she _____ surfing the Internet?

     B: Since she woke up this morning!

3. A: Does your father live in the U.S.?

     B: Yes, he _____.

     A: How long _____ he been _____ in the U.S.?

     B: He _____ in the U.S. since he _____

     25 years old.

4. A: Are you studying for the test now?

     B: Yes, I _____.

     A: How long _____ for the test?

     B: For _____.

5. A: Is your teacher teaching you the present perfect lesson?

     B: Yes, he _____.

     A: _____ long _____ you this lesson?

     B: Since _____.

(continued)

6. A: Are the students using the computers now?

 B: Yes, _____.

 A: How long _____ them?

 B: _____ they started to write their compositions.

7. A: _____ you using the Internet?

 B: Yes, I _____.

 A: How _____?

 B: _____ for two hours.

8. A: _____ your grandparents live in the U.S.?

 B: Yes, they _____.

 A: How _____ in the U.S.?

 B: Since they _____ born.

9. A: Is she studying her family history?

 B: Yes, she _____.

 A: How long _____?

 B: Since she _____.

E-Books

Before
You Read

1. Do you read a lot? What kind of books do you like to read?

2. Have you ever shopped for books on the Internet?

CD 3, TR 16

Read the following conversation. Pay special attention to the present perfect tense.

A: Do you have any hobbies?

B: Yes. I love to read.

A: How many books **have** you **read** this year?

B: **I've read** about 20 books so far this year. Last month I went on vacation for two weeks and I read 10 books while I was at the beach.

A: How did you carry so many books on your vacation? They're heavy.

B: I carried only one: my e-book. **Have** you ever **heard** of e-books?

A: No, I **haven't**. What's an e-book?

B: It's an electronic device that holds a lot of books. It can hold over 1,500 books.

A: Cool! Is it expensive?

B: The electronic device is a bit expensive. Then you have to pay to download each book. But **I've spent** a lot more money on paper books.

A: How many books **have** you **downloaded**?

B: So far **I've downloaded** about 100 books.

A: Can you get every book in electronic form?

B: One popular Web site **has made** about 250,000 books available so far. But that number is growing all the time.

A: **I've never seen** how you can download a book. Let's go to my computer and you can show me.

B: We don't need a computer. It works like a cell phone. We can download a book wherever we are.

A: Wow!

9.12 The Present Perfect with Repetition from Past to Present

We use the present perfect to talk about the repetition of an action in a time period that started in the past and includes the present. There is a probability that this action will occur again.

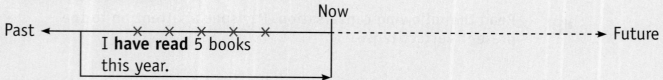

EXAMPLES	EXPLANATION
a. I **have read** 20 books this year. b. He **has downloaded** over 100 books.	a. I may read more books. b. He will probably download more books.
Up to now, one Web site **has made** about 250,000 books available. I **have read** ten chapters in my book up to now.	Adding the words "so far" and "up to now" indicate that we are counting up to the present and that more is expected.
How much money **have** you **spent** on books this year? I**'ve spent** about $500 on books this year. How many books **have** you **bought** from a bookstore this year? I **haven't bought** any books from a bookstore **at all** this year.	We can ask a question about repetition with *how much* and *how many*. To indicate zero times, we use a negative verb + *at all*. There is a probability that this action may still happen.
Compare: a. Google **had** 10,000 searches a day in 1998. b. Google **has had** billions of searches since 1998. a. Cyndi's List **appeared** for the first time in 1996. b. Many new genealogy Web sites **have appeared** in the last fifteen years.	a. We use the simple past with a time period that is finished or closed: *1998, 50 years ago, last week,* etc. b. We use the present perfect in a time period that is open. There is a probability of more repetition.

Language Note: Do not use the continuous form for repetition.
   Right: I **have downloaded** six books this year.
   Wrong: I *have been downloading* six books this year.

EXERCISE 20 **ABOUT YOU** Ask a *yes/no* question with *so far* or *up to now* and the words given. Another student will answer.

EXAMPLE   you/come to every class

A: Have you come to every class so far?
B: Yes, I have.

OR

B: No, I haven't. I've missed three classes.

1. we / have any tests
2. this lesson / be difficult
3. the teacher / give a lot of homework
4. you / understand all the explanations
5. you / have any questions about this lesson

EXERCISE 21 **ABOUT YOU** Ask a question with "*How many . . . ?*" and the words given. Talk about this month. Another student will answer.

EXAMPLE   times / go to the post office

A: How many times have you gone to the post office this month?
B: I've gone to the post office once this month.

OR

B: I haven't gone to the post office at all this month.

1. letters / write
2. times / eat in a restaurant
3. times / get paid
4. international calls / make
5. books / buy
6. times / go to the movies
7. movies / rent
8. times / cook

EXERCISE 22 **ABOUT YOU** Write four questions to ask another student or your teacher about repetition from the past to the present. Use *how much* or *how many*. The other person will answer.

EXAMPLE   How many cities have you lived in?

How many English courses have you taken at this school?

1. _____
2. _____
3. _____
4. _____

9.13 The Simple Past vs. the Present Perfect with Repetition

We use the present perfect with repetition in a present time period. There is an expectation of more repetition. We use the simple past with repetition in a past time period. There is no possibility of any more repetition during that period.

EXAMPLES	EXPLANATION
How many hits **has** your Web site **had** today? It **has had** over 100 hits today. How many times **have** you **been** absent this semester? I've **been** absent twice so far.	To show that there is an expectation of more repetition, use the present perfect. In the examples on the left, *today* and *this semester* are not finished. *So far* indicates that the number given may not be final.
Last month my Web site **had** 5,000 hits. How many times **were** you absent last semester?	The number of occurrences cannot increase in a past time frame, such as *yesterday, last week, last month, last semester,* etc. Use the simple past tense.
Brin and Page **have added** new features to Google over the years. A popular Web site **has made** thousands of e-books available.	Brin and Page are still alive. They can (and probably will) add new features to Google in the years to come. This Web site continues to make e-books available.
Before she died, my grandmother **added** many details to our family tree. My grandmother **loved** to read.	Grandmother died. Therefore, all her actions are final. Nothing can be added to them.
Compare: a. I **have checked** my e-mail twice today. b. I **checked** my e-mail twice today. a. I **have downloaded** two books this month. b. I **downloaded** two books this month.	With a present time expression (such as *today, this week, this month,* etc.), you may use either the present perfect or the simple past. In sentences (a), the number may not be final. In sentences (b), the number seems final.
Compare: a. In the U.S., I **have had** two jobs. b. In my native country, I **had** five jobs. a. In the U.S., I **have lived** in three apartments so far. b. In my native country, I **lived** in two apartments.	a. To talk about your experiences in this phase of your life, you can use the present perfect tense if there is an expectation for more. b. To talk about a closed phase of your life, use the simple past tense. For example, if you do not plan to live in your native country again, use the simple past tense to talk about your experiences there.

EXERCISE 23 **ABOUT YOU** Fill in the blanks with the simple past or the present perfect to ask a question. A student from another country will answer.

EXAMPLES How many schools __have you attended__ in the U.S.?
I've attended two schools in the U.S.

How many schools __did you attend__ in your country?
I attended only one school in my country.

1. How many apartments _____ back home?
2. How many apartments _____ here?
3. How many schools _____ in your country?
4. How many schools _____ in the U.S.?
5. How many jobs _____ in the U.S.?
6. How many jobs _____ in your country?

9.14 The Present Perfect with Indefinite Past Time

We use the present perfect to refer to an action that occurred at an indefinite time in the past that still has importance to the present situation. Words that show indefinite time are: *ever, yet,* and *already*.

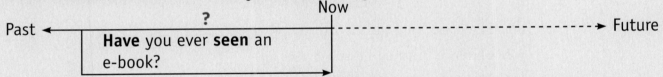

EXAMPLES	EXPLANATION

Have you **ever downloaded** a book?
    No, I **haven't.**
Have you **ever "Googled"** your own name?
    Yes, I **have.**
	A question with *ever* asks about any time between the past and the present. Put *ever* between the subject and the main verb.

Have you **finished** your book **yet**?
    No, not **yet.**
Have Larry and Sergey **become** billionaires **yet**?
    Yes, they have.
Have you **read** the story about genealogy **yet**?
    Yes, I **already** have.
	Yet and *already* refer to an indefinite time in the near past. There is an expectation that an activity took place a short time ago.

The computer **has made** it possible to do many new things. E-books **have changed** the way we read books. Cyndi Howells **has created** a very useful Web site for family historians.	We can use the present perfect to talk about the past without any reference to time. The time is not important, not known, or is imprecise. Using the present perfect, rather than the simple past, shows that the past is relevant to a present situation.

EXERCISE 24 **ABOUT YOU** **Answer the following questions with:** *Yes, I have;* *No, I haven't;* **or** *No, I never have.*

EXAMPLE Have you ever studied programming? No, I never have.

1. Have you ever "Googled" your own name?
2. Have you ever researched your family history?
3. Have you ever made a family tree?
4. Have you ever used the Web to look for a person you haven't seen in a long time?
5. Have you ever added hardware to your computer?
6. Have you ever downloaded music from the Internet?
7. Have you ever used a search engine in your native language?
8. Have you ever sent photos by e-mail?
9. Have you ever received a photo by e-mail?
10. Have you ever bought something online?
11. Have you ever built a computer?

EXERCISE 25 **ABOUT YOU** **Answer the questions.**

EXAMPLE Have we had a test on the present perfect yet? No, not yet.

1. Have you eaten lunch yet?
2. Have we finished Lesson 8 yet?
3. Have you done today's homework yet?
4. Have we written any compositions yet?
5. Have you learned the names of all the other students yet?
6. Have you visited the teacher's office yet?
7. Have we done Exercise 22 yet?
8. Have you learned the present perfect yet?
9. Have you learned all the past participles yet?

9.15 Answering a Present Perfect Question

We can answer a present perfect question with the simple past tense when a specific time is introduced in the answer. If a specific time is not known or necessary, we answer with the present perfect.

EXAMPLES	EXPLANATION
Have you ever **used** Google? **Answer A:** Yes. I've **used** Google many times. **Answer B:** Yes. I **used** Google a few hours ago.	Answer A, with *many times,* shows repetition at an indefinite time. Answer B, with *a few hours ago,* shows a specific time in the past.
Have you ever **heard** of Larry Page? **Answer A:** No. I've **never** heard of him. **Answer B:** Yes. We **read** about him yesterday.	Answer A, with *never,* shows continuation from past to present. Answer B, with *yesterday,* shows a specific time in the past.
Have you **done** your homework yet? **Answer A:** Yes. I've **done** it already. **Answer B:** Yes. I **did** it this morning.	Answer A, with *already,* is indefinite. Answer B, with *this morning,* shows a specific time.
Have Brin and Page **become** rich? **Answer A:** Yes, they **have.** **Answer B:** Yes. They **became** rich before they were 30 years old.	Answer A shows no time reference. Answer B, with *before they were 30 years old,* refers to a specific time.

EXERCISE **26** **ABOUT YOU** Ask a question with *"Have you ever . . . ?"* and the present perfect tense of the verb in parentheses ( ). Another student will answer. To answer with a specific time, use the past tense. To answer with a frequency response, use the present perfect tense. You may work with a partner.

EXAMPLES (go) to the zoo
A: Have you ever gone to the zoo?
B: Yes. I've gone there many times.

(go) to Disneyland

A: Have you ever gone to Disneyland?
B: Yes. I went there last summer.

1. (work) in a factory
2. (lose) a glove
3. (see) an e-book
4. (fall) out of bed
5. (make) a mistake in English grammar
6. (tell) a lie

7. (eat) raw[7] fish
8. (study) calculus
9. (meet) a famous person
10. (go) to an art museum
11. (download) a book
12. (break) a window
13. (buy) a book online

[7]*Raw* means not cooked.

14. (download) music

15. (go) to Las Vegas

16. (travel) by ship

17. (be) in love

18. (write) a poem

19. (send) a text message

EXERCISE 27 **ABOUT YOU** Write five questions with *ever* to ask your teacher. Your teacher will answer.

EXAMPLES

Have you *ever* gotten a parking ticket?

Have you *ever* visited Poland?

1. _____

2. _____

3. _____

4. _____

5. _____

EXERCISE 28 **ABOUT YOU** Ask a student from another country questions using the words given. The other student will answer.

EXAMPLE

your country / have a woman president

A: Has your country ever had a woman president?
B: Yes, it has. We had a woman president from 1975 to 1979.

1. your country / have a civil war

2. your country's leader / visit the U.S.

3. an American president / visit your country

4. your country / have a woman president

5. you / go back to visit your country

6. there / be an earthquake in your hometown

EXERCISE 29 **ABOUT YOU** Ask a student who has recently arrived in this country if he or she has done these things yet. The other student will answer.

EXAMPLE

buy a car

A: Have you bought a car yet?
B: Yes, I have.   OR   No, I haven't.   OR   I bought a car last month.

1. find a doctor

2. make any new friends

3. open a bank account

4. save any money

5. think about your future

6. write to your family

7. get a credit card

8. buy a computer

9. get a telephone

10. get a Social Security card

EXERCISE 30 **Fill in the blanks with the correct tense of the verb in parentheses ( ). Also fill in other missing words.**

CD 3, TR 17

A: Your Spanish is a little different from my Spanish. Where are you from?

B: I'm from Guatemala.

A: How ___long have you been___ here?
(example: you/be)

B: I _____ here for about six months. Where are you from?
(1 only/be)

A: Miami. My family comes from Cuba. They

_____ Cuba in 1962, after the revolution.
(2 leave)

I _____ born in the U.S. I'm starting
(3 be)

to become interested in my family's history.

I _____ several magazine articles about
(4 read)

genealogy so far. It's fascinating. Are you

interested in your family's history?

B: Of course I am. I _____ interested in it _____ a long time.
(5 be)   (6)

I _____ on a family tree for many years.
(7 work)

A: When _____?
(8 you/start)

B: I _____ when I _____ 16 years old. Over the years,
(9 start)   (10 be)

I _____ a lot of interesting information about my family.
(11 find)

Some of my ancestors were Mayans and some were from Spain and

France. In fact, my great-great grandfather was a Spanish prince.

A: How _____ all that information?
(12 you/find)

B: I _____ the Internet a lot. I _____ to many
(13 use)   (14 also/go)

libraries to get more information.

A: _____ to Spain or France to look at records there?
(15 you/ever/go)

B: Last summer I _____ to Spain, and I _____ a lot of
(16 go)   (17 find)

information while I was there.

A: How many ancestors _____ so far?
(18 you/find)

B: So _____ I _____ about 50, but I'm still looking.
(19)   (20 find)

(continued)

A: How can I get started?

B: There's a great Web site called Cyndi's List. I'll give you the Web address, and you can get started there.

Summary of Lesson 9

1. Compare the present perfect and the simple past.

PRESENT PERFECT	SIMPLE PAST
The action of the sentence began in the past and includes the present: now past ◄———■ - - - - - - - - ► future	The action of the sentence is completely past: now past ◄——■——| - - - - - - - - ► future
My father **has been** in the U.S. since 2002.	My father **came** to the U.S. in 2002.
My father **has had** his job in the U.S. for many years.	My father **was** in Canada for two years before he came to the U.S.
How long **have** you been interested in genealogy?	When **did** you **start** your family tree?
I**'ve** always **wanted** to learn more about my family's history.	When I was a child, I always **wanted** to spend time with my grandparents.

PRESENT PERFECT	SIMPLE PAST
Repetition from past to present: now past ◄—×××× - - - - - - - - ► future	Repetition in a past time period: now past ◄——××——| - - - - - - - - ► future
We **have had** four tests so far.	We **had** two tests last semester.
She **has used** the Internet three times today.	She **used** the Internet three times yesterday.

PRESENT PERFECT	SIMPLE PAST
The action took place at an indefinite time between the past and the present: now past ◄——?——| - - - - - - - - ► future	The action took place at a definite time in the past: now past ◄———×——| - - - - - - - - ► future
Have you ever **made** a family tree?	**Did** you **make** a family tree last month?
I**'ve done** the homework already.	I **did** the homework last night.
Have you **visited** the art museum yet?	**Did** you **visit** the art museum last month?

2. Compare the present perfect and the present perfect continuous.

PRESENT PERFECT—USE WITH:	PRESENT PERFECT CONTINUOUS—USE WITH:
A continuous action (nonaction verbs): I **have had** my car for five years.	A continuous action (action verbs): I've **been driving** a car for 20 years.
A repeated action: Cyndi's Web site **has won** several awards.	A nonstop action: The U.S. Census **has been keeping** records since the 1880s.
Question with *how many*: How many times **have** you **gone** to New York?	Question with *how long*: How long **has** he **been living** in New York?
An action that is at an indefinite time, completely in the past: Cyndi **has created** a Web site.	An action that started in the past and is still happening: Cyndi **has been working** on her family history since 1992.

Editing Advice

1. Don't confuse the *-ing* form and the past participle.

      taking
She has been ~~taken~~ a test for two hours.

    given
She has ~~giving~~ him a present.

2. Use the present perfect, not the simple present, to describe an action or state that started in the past and continues to the present.

    had
He has a car for two years.
      ^

    have   *ed*
How long ~~do~~ you work in a factory?
                 ^

3. Use *for*, not *since*, with the amount of time.

                          for
I've been studying English ~~since~~ three months.

4. Use the simple past, not the present perfect, with a specific past time.

    came
He ~~has come~~ to the U.S. five months ago.

    did
When ~~have~~ you come to the U.S.?

5. Use the simple past, not the present perfect, in a *since* clause.

> *came*
> He has learned a lot of English since he ~~has come~~ to the U.S.

6. Use the correct word order. Put the adverb between the auxiliary and the main verb.

> *never seen*
> He has ~~seen never~~ a French movie.

> *ever gone*
> Have you ~~gone ever~~ to France?

7. Use the correct word order in questions.

> *have you*
> How long ~~you have~~ been a teacher?

8. Use *yet* for negative statements; use *already* for affirmative statements.

> *yet*
> I haven't eaten dinner ~~already~~.

9. Don't forget the verb *have* in the present perfect (continuous).

> *have*
> I ʌ been living in New York for two years.

10. Don't forget the *-ed* of the past participle.

> *ed*
> He's listen ʌ to that CD many times.

11. Use the present perfect, not the continuous form, with *always, never, yet, already, ever,* and *how many*.

> *gone*
> How many times have you ~~been going~~ to Paris?

> *visited*
> I've never ~~been visiting~~ Paris.

12. Don't use *time* after *how long*.

> How long ~~time~~ have you had your job?

Editing Quiz

Some of the shaded words and phrases have mistakes. Find the mistakes and correct them. If the shaded words are correct, write C.

have you   *C*
"How many changes ~~you have~~ made since you came to the U.S.?" For our
(example)   *(example)*

journal, our teacher asked us to answer this question. I have come to the
(1)

U.S. two and a half years ago. Things have changing a lot for me since
(2)

I've come to the U.S. Here's a list of some of the changes:
(3)

1. Since the past two years I am studying English. I knew a little English
   (4)   *(5)*   *(6)*

   before I came here, but my English has improve a lot.
   (7)   *(8)*

2. Now I have a driver's permit and I'm learning how to drive. I haven't took
   (9)

   the driver's test yet because I'm not ready. I haven't practiced enough
   (10)

   already.
   (11)

3. I've been eaten a lot of different foods like hamburgers and pizza.
   (12)

   I never ate those in my country. Unfortunately, I been gaining weight.
   (13)   *(14)*

4. I started to work in a factory three months ago. Since I have started
   (15)   *(16)*   *(17)*

   my job, I haven't have much time for fun.
   (18)

5. I've gone to several museums in this city. But I've taken never a trip to
   (19)   *(20)*

   another American city. I'd like to visit New York, but I haven't saved
   (21)

   enough money yet.
   (22)

6. I've been living in three apartments so far. In my country, I lived in
   (23)   *(24)*

   a house with my family.

7. I've answered the following questions about a thousand times so far:
   (25)

   "Where do you come from?" and "How long time you have been in
   (26)   *(27)*

   the U.S.?" I'm getting tired of always answering the same question.

Lesson 9 Test/Review

PART 1 Fill in the blanks with the simple past, the present perfect, or the present perfect continuous form by using the words in parentheses ( ). In some cases, more than one answer is possible.

Conversation 1

A: ___Have___ you ever ___studied___ computer programming?
(example: study)

B: Yes. I _____ it in college. And I _____ as a programmer
        (1 study)   (2 work)
for five years. But my job is boring.

A: _____ you ever _____ about changing jobs?
                          (3 think)

B: Yes. Since I _____ a child, I _____ to be an
                    (4 be)   (5 always/want)
actor. When I was in college, I _____ in a few plays, but
                                (6 be)

since I _____, I _____ time to act.
        (7 graduate)   (8 not/have)

Conversation 2

A: How long _____ in the U.S.?
                  (1 you/be)

B: For about two years.

A: _____ a lot since you _____ to the U.S.?
       (2 your life/change)   (3 come)

B: Oh, yes. Before I _____ here, I _____ with my family.
                         (4 come)   (5 live)
Since I came here, I _____ alone.
                     (6 live)

A: _____ in the same apartment in this city?
       (7 always/live)

B: No. I _____ three times so far. And I plan to move again at
            (8 move)
the end of the year.

A: Do you plan to have a roommate?

B: Yes, but I _____ one yet.
                  (9 not/find)

PART 2 **Fill in the blanks with the simple present, the simple past, the present perfect, or the present perfect continuous form of the verb in parentheses ( ). In some cases, more than one answer is possible.**

Paragraph 1

I _____ the Internet every day. I _____ it for many years.
(1 use)   (2 use)

I _____ to use it when I _____ interested in genealogy.
(3 start)   (4 become)

I _____ on my family tree for three years. Last month,
(5 work)

I _____ information about my father's ancestors. My grandfather
(6 find)

_____ with us now and likes to tell us about his past. He _____
(7 live)   (8 be)

born in Italy, but he _____ here when he was very young, so he
(9 come)

_____ here most of his life. He doesn't remember much about Italy.
(10 live)

I _____ any information about my mother's ancestors yet.
(11 not/find)

Paragraph 2

I _____ to the U.S. when a war _____ out in my country.
(1 come)   (2 break)

I _____ in the U.S. for five years. At first, everything
(3 live)

_____ very hard for me. I _____ any English when
(4 be)   (5 not/know)

I _____. But I _____ English for the past five years,
(6 arrive)   (7 study)

and now I _____ it pretty well. I _____ my college
(8 speak)   (9 not/start)

education yet, but I plan to next semester.

Expansion

Classroom Activities

1 **Form a group of between four and six students. Find out who in your group has done each of these things. Write that person's name in the blank.**

a. _____ has made a family tree.

b. _____ has found a good job.

c. _____ has been on a ship.

d. _____ has never eaten Mexican food.

e. _____ hasn't done today's homework yet.

f. _____ has never seen a French movie.

g. _____ has taken a trip to Canada.

h. _____ has acted in a play.

i. _____ has gone swimming in the Pacific Ocean.

j. _____ has flown in a helicopter.

k. _____ has served in the military.

l. _____ has worked in a hotel.

m. _____ has never studied chemistry.

n. _____ has taken the TOEFL[8] test.

o. _____ has just gotten a "green card."

p. _____ has downloaded music from the Internet.

2 **Draw your family tree for the past three generations, if you can. Form a small group and tell the others in your group a little about your family.**

Talk About It

1 **Why do you think so many people are interested in genealogy? What is valuable about finding your family's history?**

2 **What are the advantages of an e-book over a paper book? What are the disadvantages?**

3 **Do you think people spend too much time surfing the Internet?**

---

[8]The *TOEFL*™ is the Test of English as a Foreign Language. Many U.S. colleges and universities require foreign students to take this test.

Write

About It

❶ Write about new technology that you've started using recently. How has that made your life different?

❷ Write a composition about one of the following:

How your life has changed since (*choose one*):

a. you came to the U.S.

b. you got married

c. you had a baby

d. you graduated from high school

e. you started to study here

Changes in My Life

My life has changed a lot since I started college. When I was in high school, I didn't have many responsibilities. Since I started college, I've had to work and study at the same time. When I was in high school, I used to hang out with my friends. Now that I'm in college, I haven't had much time for my friends . . .

 For more practice using grammar in context, please visit our Web site.

Lesson

10

Grammar
Gerunds

Infinitives

Context
Finding a Job

10.1 Gerunds—An Overview

To form a gerund, we use the *-ing* form of a verb (*finding, learning, eating, running*). A *gerund phrase* is a gerund + a noun phrase (*finding a job, learning English*). A gerund (phrase) can appear in several positions in a sentence.

EXAMPLES	EXPLANATION
a. **Finding** a job is hard. b. I don't enjoy **talking** about myself. c. I thought about **changing** my career. d. I got help **by talking** with my counselor. e. I like to **go shopping**.	a. The gerund is the subject. b. The gerund is the object. c. The gerund is the object of the preposition. d. The gerund is part of an adverbial phrase. e. The gerund is in many expressions with *go*.
Not having a job is frustrating. You can impress the boss by **not being** late.	We can put *not* in front of a gerund to make it negative.

Finding a Job

Before You Read

1. Have you ever had a job interview in this city?

2. What is your profession or job? What profession or job do you plan to have in the future?

CD 3, TR 18

Read the following Web article. Pay special attention to gerunds.

http://www.website*reading.com

Finding a job in the United States takes specific skills. The following advice will help you find a job.

- Write a good résumé. Describe your accomplishments.[1] Avoid **including** unnecessary information. Your résumé should be one page, if possible.
- Find out about available jobs. One way is by **looking** in the newspaper or on the Internet. Another way is by **networking**. **Networking** means **exchanging** information with anyone you know—family, friends, neighbors, classmates, former coworkers, professional groups—who might know of a job. These people might also be able to give you insider information about a company, such as who is in charge and what it is like to work at their company. According to an article in

[1]*Accomplishments* are the unusual good things you have done, such as awards you have won or projects you have successfully managed.

the *Wall Street Journal*, 94 percent of people who succeed in **finding** a job say that **networking** was a big help.

- Practice the interview. The more prepared you are, the more relaxed you will feel. If you are worried about **saying** or **doing** the wrong thing, practice will help.
- Learn something about the company. You can find information by **going** to the company's Web site. **Getting** information takes time, but it pays off.

You can get help in these skills—**writing** a résumé, **networking**, **preparing** for an interview, **researching** a company—by **seeing** a career counselor. Most high schools and colleges have one who can help you get started.

Finding a job is one of the most difficult jobs. Some people send out hundreds of résumés and go on dozens of interviews before **finding** a job. And it isn't something you do just once or twice in your lifetime. For most Americans, **changing** jobs many times in a lifetime is not uncommon.

Tips For Getting a Job

Preparation:
1. Learn about the organization and have a specific job or jobs in mind.
2. Review your résumé.
3. Practice an interview with a friend or relative.
4. Arrive at least 15 minutes before the scheduled time of your interview.

Personal appearance:
1. Be well-groomed[2] and dress appropriately.
2. Do not chew gum.

The interview:
1. Relax and answer each question concisely.
2. Use good manners. Shake hands and smile when you meet someone.
3. Be enthusiastic. Tell the interviewer why you are a good candidate for the job.
4. Ask questions about the position and the organization.
5. Thank the interviewer when you leave and in writing as a follow-up.

Information to bring to an interview:
1. Social Security card.
2. Government-issued identification (driver's license).
3. Résumé or application. Include information about your education, training, and previous employment.
4. References. Employers typically require three references. Get permission before using anyone as a reference. Make sure that each will give you a good reference. Avoid using relatives as references.

[2]When you are *well-groomed*, your appearance is neat and clean.

10.2 Gerund as Subject

EXAMPLES	EXPLANATION
Gerund Phrase **Finding a good job** takes time. **Writing a résumé** isn't easy. **Not preparing** for an interview could have a bad result.	We can use a gerund or gerund phrase as the subject of the sentence.
Exchanging ideas with friends **is** helpful. **Visiting** company Web sites **takes** time.	A gerund subject takes a singular verb.

EXERCISE 1 The following things are important before a job interview. Make a sentence with each one, using a gerund phrase as the subject.

EXAMPLE   get a good night's sleep

Getting a good night's sleep will help you feel rested and alert for

an interview.

1. take a bath or shower

_____

2. select serious-looking clothes

_____

3. prepare a résumé

_____

4. check your résumé carefully

_____

5. get information about the company

_____

6. prepare answers to possible questions

_____

EXERCISE 2 Complete each statement with a gerund (phrase) as the subject.

EXAMPLE   _____ *Learning a foreign language* _____ takes a long time.

1. _____ is one of the most difficult jobs.

2. _____ is one of the best ways to find a job.

3. _____ is not permitted in this classroom.

4. _____ is difficult for a foreign student.

5. _____ takes a long time.

6. _____ is not polite.

EXERCISE **3** **ABOUT YOU** In preparing for an interview, it is good to think about the following questions. Answer these questions. Use a gerund in some of your answers, but do *not* try to use a gerund in every answer. It won't work. Give a lot of thought to your answers and compare them with your classmates' answers.

EXAMPLES What are your strengths?
Working with others; learning quickly; thinking fast in difficult situations

What are your strong and weak subjects in school?
I'm strong in math. I'm weak in history.

1. What are your strengths?

_____

2. What are some of your weaknesses?

_____

3. List your accomplishments and achievements. (They can be achievements in jobs, sports, school, etc.)

_____

4. What are your interests?

_____

5. What are your short-term goals?

_____

6. What are your long-term goals?

_____

7. What are some things you like? Think about personalities, tasks, environments, types of work, and structure.

_____

8. What are some things you dislike? Think about personalities, tasks, environments, types of work, and structure.

_____

9. Why should we hire you?

_____

EXERCISE 4 Write a list of personal behaviors during an interview that would hurt your chances of getting a job. You may work with a partner or in a small group.

EXAMPLES   Chewing gum during the interview looks bad.

Not looking directly at the interviewer can hurt your chances.

1. _____
2. _____
3. _____
4. _____
5. _____

10.3 Gerund after Verb

Some verbs are commonly followed by a gerund (phrase). The gerund (phrase) is the object of the verb.

EXAMPLES	EXPLANATION
Have you **considered going** to a job counselor? Do you **appreciate getting** advice? You can **discuss improving** your skills. You should **practice answering** interview questions. If you don't find a job immediately, **keep trying**.	The verbs below can be followed by a gerund: admit — discuss — mind — put off appreciate — dislike — miss — quit avoid — enjoy — permit — recommend can't help — finish — postpone — risk consider — keep — practice — suggest
I have many hobbies: I like to **go fishing** in the summer. I **go skiing** in the winter. I like indoor sports too. I **go bowling** once a month.	*Go* + gerund is used in many idiomatic expressions. go boating — go jogging go bowling — go sailing go camping — go shopping go dancing — go sightseeing go fishing — go skating go hiking — go skiing go hunting — go swimming
a. I don't **mind wearing** a suit to work. b. Don't **put off writing** your résumé. Do it now. c. I have an interview tomorrow morning. I **can't help feeling** nervous.	a. *I mind* means that something bothers me. *I don't mind* means that something is OK with me; it doesn't bother me. b. *Put off* means postpone. c. *Can't help* means to have no control over something.

EXERCISE **5** **ABOUT YOU** Fill in the blanks with an appropriate gerund (or noun) to complete these statements. Share your answers with the class.

EXAMPLE   I don't mind ___shopping for food___, but I do[3] mind ___cooking it___.

1. I usually enjoy _____ during the summer.

2. I don't enjoy _____.

3. I don't mind _____, but I do mind _____.

4. I appreciate _____ from my friends.

5. I need to practice _____ if I want to improve.

6. I often put off _____.

7. I need to keep _____ if I want to be successful.

8. I should avoid _____ if I want to improve my health.

9. I miss _____ from my hometown.

EXERCISE **6** **ABOUT YOU** Make a list of suggestions and recommendations for a tourist who is about to visit your hometown. Read your list to a partner, a small group, or the entire class.

EXAMPLES   I recommend taking warm clothes for the winter.

You should avoid drinking tap water.

1. I recommend:

_____

_____

_____

2. You should avoid:

_____

_____

_____

EXERCISE **7** **ABOUT YOU** Tell if you like or don't like the following activities. Explain why.

EXAMPLES   go hunting
I don't like to go hunting because I don't like to kill animals.

go bowling
I like to go bowling because I think it's a fun activity.

1. go fishing   3. go jogging   5. go hunting

2. go camping   4. go swimming   6. go shopping

[3]*Do* makes the verb more emphatic. In this sentence, it shows contrast with *don't mind*.

10.4 Gerund after Preposition[4]

A gerund can follow a preposition. It is important to choose the correct preposition after a verb or adjective.

PREPOSITION COMBINATIONS		COMMON COMBINATIONS	EXAMPLES
Verb + Preposition	verb + *about*	care about complain about dream about forget about talk about think about worry about	I **care about doing** well in an interview. My sister **dreams about becoming** a doctor.
	verb + *to*	adjust to look forward to object to	I **look forward to getting** a job and **saving** money.
	verb + *on*	depend on insist on plan on	I **plan on going** to a career counselor.
	verb + *in*	believe in succeed in	My father **succeeded in finding** a good job.
Adjective + Preposition	adjective + *of*	afraid of capable of guilty of proud of tired of	I'm **afraid of losing** my job.
	adjective + *about*	concerned about excited about upset about worried about sad about	He is **upset about not getting** the job.
	adjective + *for*	responsible for famous for grateful to . . . for	Who is **responsible for hiring** in this company?
	adjective + *at*	good at successful at	I'm not very **good at writing** a résumé.
	adjective + *to*	accustomed to used to	I'm not **accustomed to talking** about my strengths.
	adjective + *in*	interested in successful in	Are you **interested in getting** a better job?

(continued)

[4]For a list of verbs and adjectives followed by a preposition, see Appendix H.

Language Notes:
1. *Plan, afraid,* and *proud* can be followed by an infinitive too.
   I plan **on seeing** a counselor. / I plan **to see** a counselor.
   I'm afraid **of losing** my job. / I'm afraid **to lose** my job.
   He's proud **of being** a college graduate. / He's proud **to be** a college graduate.
2. Notice that in some expressions, *to* is a preposition followed by a gerund, not part of an infinitive.

Compare:
   I need **to write** a résumé. (infinitive)
   I'm not accustomed **to writing** a résumé. (*to* + gerund)

EXERCISE 8   **ABOUT YOU**   **Complete the questions with a gerund (phrase). Then ask another student these questions.**

EXAMPLE   Are you lazy about *doing your homework?* _____

1. Do you ever worry about _____
2. Do you plan on _____
3. Do you ever think about _____
4. When you get tired of _____, what do you do?
5. Are you interested in _____

EXERCISE 9   **ABOUT YOU**   **Fill in the blanks with a preposition and a gerund (phrase) to make a true statement.**

EXAMPLE   I plan *on going back to Haiti soon.* _____

1. I'm afraid _____
2. I'm not afraid _____
3. I'm interested _____
4. I'm not interested _____
5. I want to succeed _____
6. I'm not very good _____
7. I'm accustomed _____
8. I'm not accustomed _____
9. I plan _____
10. I don't care _____

EXERCISE 10 **ABOUT YOU** Fill in the blanks with a gerund or noun phrase to complete each statement. Compare your experiences in the U.S. with your experiences in your native country. You may share your answers with a small group or with the entire class.

EXAMPLES   In the U.S., I'm afraid of _walking alone at night._

In my native country, I was afraid of _not being able to get a good_ _education._

1. In the U.S., I'm interested in _____

   In my native country, I was interested in _____

   _____

2. In the U.S., I worry about _____

   In my native country, I worried about _____

   _____

3. In the U.S., I dream about _____

   In my native country, I dreamed about _____

   _____

4. In the U.S., I look forward to _____

   In my native country, I looked forward to _____

   _____

5. In the U.S., people often complain about _____

   In my native country, people often complain about _____

   _____

6. In the U.S., families often talk about _____

   In my native country, families often talk about _____

   _____

7. American students are accustomed to _____

   Students in my native country are accustomed to _____

   _____

10.5 Gerund in Adverbial Phrase

EXAMPLES	EXPLANATION
You should practice interview questions **before going** on an interview. I found my job **by looking** in the newspaper. She took the test **without studying**.	We can use a gerund in an adverbial phrase that begins with a preposition: *before*, *by*, *after*, *without*, etc.

EXERCISE 11   **Fill in the blanks to complete the sentences. Practice using gerunds.**

EXAMPLE   The best way to improve your vocabulary is by _____ reading.

1. One way to find a job is by _____

2. It is very difficult to find a job without _____
_____

3. The best way to improve your pronunciation is by _____
_____

4. The best way to quit a bad habit is by _____

5. One way to find an apartment is by _____

6. I can't speak English without _____

7. It's impossible to get a driver's license without _____
_____

8. You should read the instructions for a test before _____
_____

EXERCISE 12   **Fill in the blanks in the conversation below with the gerund form. Where you see two blanks, use a preposition before the gerund. Answers may vary.**

CD 3, TR 19

A: I need to find a job. I've had ten interviews, but so far no job.

B: Have you thought ___about___ ___going___ to a job counselor?
          (example)   (example)

A: No. Where can I find one?

B: Our school office has a counseling department. I suggest
_____ an appointment with a counselor.
      (1)

A: What can a job counselor do for me?

B: Do you know anything about interviewing skills?

A: No.

B: Well, with the job counselor, you can talk _____ (2)

_____ a good impression during an interview.
(3)

You can practice _____ questions that the interviewer
(4)

might ask you.

A: Really? How does the counselor know what questions the interviewer

will ask me?

B: Many interviewers ask the same general questions. For example, the

interviewer might ask you, "Do you enjoy _____
(5)

with computers?" Or she might ask you, "Do you mind

_____ overtime and on weekends?" Or "Are you
(6)

good _____ _____ with other people?"
(7)   (8)

A: I dislike _____ about myself.
(9)

B: That's what you have to do in the U.S.

A: What else can the counselor help me with?

B: If your skills are low, you can talk _____
(10)

_____ your skills. If you don't know much about
(11)

computers, for example, she can recommend _____
(12)

more classes.

A: It feels like I'm never going to find a job. I'm tired _____
(13)

_____ and not finding anything.
(14)

B: If you keep _____ , you will succeed _____
(15)   (16)

_____ a job. I'm sure. But it takes time and patience.
(17)

10.6 Infinitives—An Overview

To form an infinitive, we use *to* + the base form of a verb (*to find, to help, to run, to be*).

EXAMPLES	EXPLANATION
I want **to find** a job.	An infinitive is used after certain verbs.
I want you **to help** me.	An object can be added before an infinitive.
I'm happy **to help** you.	An infinitive can follow certain adjectives.
It's important **to write** a good résumé.	An infinitive follows certain expressions with *it*.
He went to a counselor **to get** advice.	An infinitive is used to show purpose.

Tips[5] on Writing a Résumé

Before You Read

1. Have you ever written a résumé? What is the hardest part about writing a résumé?

2. Do people in your native country have to write a résumé?

CD 3, TR 20

Read the following Web article. Pay special attention to infinitives.

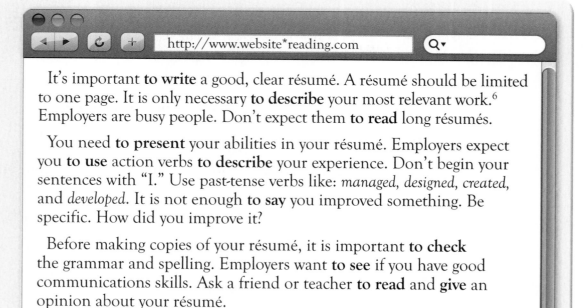

http://www.website*reading.com

It's important **to write** a good, clear résumé. A résumé should be limited to one page. It is only necessary **to describe** your most relevant work.[6] Employers are busy people. Don't expect them **to read** long résumés.

You need **to present** your abilities in your résumé. Employers expect you **to use** action verbs **to describe** your experience. Don't begin your sentences with "I." Use past-tense verbs like: *managed, designed, created,* and *developed*. It is not enough **to say** you improved something. Be specific. How did you improve it?

Before making copies of your résumé, it is important **to check** the grammar and spelling. Employers want **to see** if you have good communications skills. Ask a friend or teacher **to read** and **give** an opinion about your résumé.

[5]A *tip* is a small piece of advice.
[6]*Relevant work* is work that is related to this particular job opening.

It isn't necessary **to include** references. If the employer wants you **to provide** references, he or she will ask you **to do** so during or after the interview.

Don't include personal information such as marital status, age, race, family information, or hobbies.

Be honest in your résumé. Employers can check your information. No one wants **to hire** a liar.

TINA WHITE

1234 Anderson Avenue
West City, MA 01766
tina.white@e*mail.com
617-123-1234

EXPERIENCE

COMPUTER SALES MANAGER
Acme Computer Services, Inc., Concord, MA
March 2003–Present
- Managed computer services department, overseeing 20 sales representatives throughout New England.
- Exceeded annual sales goal by 20 percent in 2008.
- Created online customer database, enabling representatives and company to track and retain customers and improve service.
- Developed new training program and materials for all company sales representatives.

OFFICE MANAGER
West Marketing Services, West City, MA
June 1999–March 2003
- Implemented new system for improving accounting records and reports.
- Managed, trained, and oversaw five customer service representatives.
- Grew sales contracts for support services by 200 percent in first two years.

EDUCATION AND TRAINING
Northeastern Community College, Salem, MA
   Associates Degree Major: Accounting
Institute of Management, Boston, MA
   Certificate of Completion. Course: Sales Management

COMPUTER SKILLS
   Proficient in use of MS Windows, PowerPoint, Excel, Access, Outlook, Mac OS X, and several accounting and database systems.

10.7 Infinitive as Subject

An infinitive can be the subject of a sentence. We begin the sentence with *it* and delay the infinitive subject.

EXAMPLES	EXPLANATION
It is important **to write** a good résumé. It isn't necessary **to include** all your experience.	We can use an infinitive after these adjectives: dangerous good necessary difficult hard possible easy important sad expensive impossible wrong
It takes time **to prepare** for an interview. It takes patience **to find** a job. It costs money **to use** a résumé service.	We can use an infinitive after certain nouns. time patience money fun a pleasure experience
It is necessary **for the manager to choose** the best candidate for the job. It isn't easy **for me to talk** about myself. It was hard **for her to leave** her last job.	Include *for* + noun or object pronoun to make a statement that is true of a specific person.
Compare Infinitive and Gerund Subjects: It's important **to arrive** on time. **Arriving** on time is important.	There is no difference in meaning between an infinitive subject and a gerund subject.

EXERCISE 13   **Fill in the blanks with an appropriate infinitive to give information about résumés and interviews. Answers may vary.**

EXAMPLE   It is necessary _____*to have*_____ a Social Security card.

1. It isn't necessary _____ all your previous experience. Choose only the most relevant experience.

2. It's important _____ your spelling and grammar before sending a résumé.

3. It is a good idea _____ interview questions before going on an interview.

4. It is important _____ your best when you go on an interview, so choose your clothes carefully.

5. It isn't necessary _____ references on a résumé. You can simply write, "References available upon request."

6. It's important _____ your past work experience in detail, using words like *managed, designed, supervised,* and *built.*

7. It takes time _____ a good résumé.

EXERCISE 14 **Complete each statement with an infinitive phrase. You can add an object, if you like.**

EXAMPLES   It's easy ___to shop in an American supermarket.___

It's necessary ___for me to pay my rent by the fifth of the month.___

1. It's important _____
2. It's impossible _____
3. It's possible _____
4. It's necessary _____
5. It's dangerous _____
6. It isn't good _____
7. It's expensive _____
8. It's hard _____

EXERCISE 15 **ABOUT YOU** **Tell if it's important or not important for you to do the following.**

EXAMPLE   own a house
It's (not) important for me to own a house.

1. get a college degree
2. find an interesting job
3. have a car
4. speak English well
5. read and write English well
6. study American history
7. become an American citizen
8. own a computer
9. have a cell phone
10. make a lot of money

EXERCISE 16 **Write a sentence with each pair of words below. You may read your sentences to the class.**

EXAMPLE   hard / the teacher

___It's hard for the teacher to pronounce the names of some students.___

1. important / us (the students)

_____

2. difficult / Americans

_____

3. easy / the teacher

_____

4. necessary / children

_____

5. difficult / a woman

_____

6. difficult / a man

_____

EXERCISE 17   **Write a list of things that a foreign student or immigrant should know about life in the U.S. Use gerunds or infinitives as subjects. You may work with a partner.**

EXAMPLES   It is possible for some students to get financial aid. _____

Learning English is going to take longer than you expected. _____

1. _____

2. _____

3. _____

4. _____

5. _____

6. _____

10.8 Infinitive after Adjective

Some adjectives can be followed by an infinitive.

EXAMPLES	EXPLANATION
I would be **happy to help** you with your résumé. Are you **prepared to make** copies of your résumé?	Adjectives often followed by an infinitive are: afraid happy prepared ready glad lucky proud sad

EXERCISE 18 Complete this conversation with appropriate infinitives. Answers may vary.

CD 3, TR 21

A: I have my first interview tomorrow. I'm afraid ___*to go*___
(example)
alone. Would you go with me?

B: I'd be happy _____ with you and wait in the
_(1)_
car. But nobody can go with you on an interview.
You have to do it alone. It sounds like you're not
ready _____ a job interview. You should see
_(2)_
a job counselor and get some practice before you
have an interview. I was lucky _____ a great job counselor.
_(3)_
She prepared me well.

A: I don't have time to make an appointment with a job counselor
before tomorrow. Maybe you can help me.

B: I'd be happy _____ you. Do you have some time this afternoon?
_(4)_
We can go over some basic questions.

A: Thanks. I'm glad _____ you as my friend.
_(5)_

B: That's what friends are for.

EXERCISE 19   **ABOUT YOU** Fill in the blanks.

EXAMPLE   I'm lucky ___*to be in the U.S.*_____

1. I was lucky _____
2. I'm proud _____
3. I'm sometimes afraid _____
4. I'm not afraid _____
5. In the U.S., I'm afraid _____
6. Are we ready _____
7. I'm not prepared _____

10.9 Infinitive after Verb

Some verbs are commonly followed by an infinitive (phrase).

EXAMPLES	EXPLANATION
I need **to find** a new job. I decided **to quit** my old job. I prefer **to work** outdoors. I want **to make** more money.	We can use an infinitive after the following verbs: agree decide like promise ask expect love remember attempt forget need start begin hope plan try continue learn prefer want

Pronunciation Note: The *to* in infinitives is often pronounced "ta" or, after a *d* sound, "da." *Want to* is often pronounced "wanna." Listen to your teacher pronounce the sentences in the above box.

EXERCISE 20 **ABOUT YOU** Ask a question with the words given in the present tense. Another student will answer.

EXAMPLE like / work in an office

> **A:** Do you like to work in an office?
> **B:** Yes, I do. OR No, I don't.

1. plan / look for a job
2. expect / make a lot of money at your next job
3. like / work with computers
4. prefer / work the second shift
5. need / see a job counselor
6. hope / become rich some day
7. like / work with people
8. try / keep up with changes in technology
9. want / learn another language

EXERCISE 21 **ABOUT YOU** Write a sentence about yourself using the words given, in any tense. You may share your sentences with the class.

EXAMPLES like / eat
I like to eat Chinese food. _____

try / find
I'm trying to find a job. _____

1. like / read

   _____

2. not like / eat

   _____

3. want / visit

   _____

4. decide / go

   _____

5. try / learn

   _____

6. begin / study

   _____

EXERCISE 22 **ABOUT YOU** Check (✓) the activities that you like to do. Tell the class why you like or don't like this activity.

1. ____ stay home on the weekends
2. ____ eat in a restaurant
3. ____ get up early
4. ____ talk on the phone
5. ____ surf the Internet
6. ____ go to the library
7. ____ swim

8. ____ go to museums
9. ____ dance
10. ____ write letters
11. ____ play chess
12. ____ watch sports on TV
13. ____ read
14. ____ go shopping

10.10 Gerund or Infinitive after Verb

Some verbs can be followed by either a gerund or an infinitive with almost no difference in meaning.

EXAMPLES	EXPLANATION
I started **looking** for a job a month ago. I started **to look** for a job a month ago. He continued **working** until he was 65 years old. He continued **to work** until he was 65 years old.	The verbs below can be followed by either a gerund or an infinitive with almost no difference in meaning: attempt deserve prefer begin hate start can't stand[7] like try continue love

Language Notes:

1. The meaning of *try* + infinitive is a little different from the meaning of *try* + gerund.
   Try + infinitive means to make an effort.
   I'll **try to improve** my résumé.
   You should **try to relax** during the interview.
2. *Try* + gerund means to use a different technique when one technique doesn't produce the result you want.
   I wanted to reach you yesterday, but I couldn't. I **tried calling** your home phone, but I got your answering machine. I **tried calling** your cell phone, but it was turned off. I **tried e-mailing** you, but you didn't check your e-mail.

EXERCISE 23   **ABOUT YOU**   Complete each statement using either a gerund (phrase) or an infinitive (phrase). Practice both ways.

EXAMPLES   I started ___to learn English four years ago___.
                                  (learn)

          I started ___studying French when I was in high school___.
                                  (study)

1. I started _____ to this school in _____.
                   (come)

2. I began _____ English _____.
              (study)

3. I like _____ on TV.
                             (watch)

4. I like _____.
                               (live)

5. I hate _____.
                               (wear)

6. I love _____.
                               (eat)

[7]*Can't stand* means hate or can't tolerate. I *can't stand* waiting in a long line.

10.11 Object before Infinitive

We can use a noun or object pronoun (*me, you, him, her, it, us,* and *them*) before an infinitive.

EXAMPLES	EXPLANATION
Don't **expect an employer to read** a long résumé. I **want you to look** at my résumé. My boss **wants me to work** overtime. I **expected him to give** me a raise.	We often use an object between the following verbs and an infinitive: advise invite want allow need would like ask permit expect tell
He helped me **find** a job. He helped me *to* **find** a job.	*Help* can be followed by either an object + base form or an object + infinitive.

EXERCISE 24   **Fill in the blanks with pronouns and infinitives to complete the conversation below.**

CD 3, TR 22

A: I want to quit my job.

B: Why?

A: I don't like my supervisor. He expects ___**me**___ ___**to work**___
(example) (example: work)
at night and on weekends.

B: But you get extra pay for that, don't you?

A: No. I asked _____ _____ me a raise, but he said the
(1)   (2 give)
company can't afford it.

B: Is that the only problem?

A: No. My coworkers and I like to go out for lunch. But he doesn't

want _____ _____ out. He expects _____ _____
(3)   (4 go)   (5)   (6 eat)
in the company cafeteria. He says that if we go out, we might not get

back on time.

B: That's awful. He should permit _____ _____ wherever you
(7)   (8 eat)
want to.

A: That's what I think. I also have a problem with my manager.

She never gives anyone a compliment. When I do a good

job, I expect _____ _____ something nice.
(9)   (10 say)
But she only says something when we make a mistake.

(continued)

B: It's important to get positive feedback too.

A: Do you know of any jobs in your company? I'd like

_____(11)_____ _____(12 ask)_____ your boss if he

needs anyone.

B: I don't think there are any job openings in my company. My boss

has two sons in their twenties. He wants _____(13)_____

_____(14 work)_____ for him on Saturdays. But they're so

lazy. The boss allows _____(15)_____ _____(16 come)_____

late and _____(17 leave)_____ early. He would never permit

_____(18)_____ _____(19 do)_____ that. We have to be

on time exactly, or he'll take away some of our pay.

A: Maybe I should just stay at my job. I guess no job is perfect.

EXERCISE **25** **Tell if the teacher wants or doesn't want the students to do the following.**

EXAMPLES do the homework
The teacher wants us to do the homework.

use the textbook during a test
The teacher doesn't want us to use the textbook during a test.

1. talk to another student during a test

2. study before a test

3. copy another student's homework in class

4. learn English

5. speak our native languages in class

6. improve our pronunciation

7. talk about our native countries in class

8. sit in rows

EXERCISE `26` **ABOUT YOU** Tell if you expect or don't expect the teacher to do the following.

EXAMPLES give homework
I expect him/her to give homework.

give me private lessons
I don't expect him/her to give me private lessons.

1. correct the homework
2. give tests
3. speak my native language
4. help me after class
5. come to class on time

6. pass all the students
7. know a lot about my native country
8. answer my questions in class
9. teach us American history
10. pronounce my name correctly

EXERCISE `27` **ABOUT YOU** Write sentences to tell what one member of your family wants (or doesn't want) from another member of your family.

EXAMPLES *My father doesn't want my brother to watch so much TV.*

My brother wants me to help him with his math homework.

1. _____
2. _____
3. _____
4. _____

10.12 Infinitive to Show Purpose

We use the infinitive to show purpose.

EXAMPLES	EXPLANATION
You can use the Internet **in order to find** job information. I need a car **in order to get** to work. I'm saving my money **in order to buy** a car.	*In order to* + verb shows purpose.
You can use the Internet **to find** job information. I need a car **to get** to work. I'm saving my money **to buy** a car.	*To* is the short form of *in order to*.

EXERCISE 28 **Fill in the blanks with an infinitive to show purpose. Answers will vary.**

EXAMPLE   I bought the Sunday newspaper _to look for a job_.

1. I called the company _____ an appointment.

2. She wants to work overtime _____.

3. You should use the Internet _____ jobs.

4. You can use a résumé writing service _____ your résumé.

5. My interview is in a distant suburb. I need a car _____ the interview.

6. Use express mail _____ packages faster.

7. In the U.S., you need experience _____ a job, and you need a job _____ experience.

8. I need two phone lines. I need one _____ on the phone with my friends and relatives. I need the other one _____ business calls.

9. I'm sending an envelope that has a lot of papers in it. I need extra stamps _____ this envelope.

10. You should go to the college admissions office _____ _____ a copy of your transcripts.

11. After an interview, you can call the employer _____ _____ that you're very interested in the position.

Rita's Story

Before You Read

1. What are some differences between the American workplace and the workplace in other countries?

2. In your native culture, is it a sign of respect or disrespect to look at someone directly?

Read the following journal entry. Pay special attention to *used to,* *be used to,* and *get used to.*

August 23

I've been in the U.S. for two years. I **used to** study British English in India, so I had a hard time **getting used to** the American pronunciation. But little by little, I started to **get used to** it. Now I understand Americans well, and they understand me.

I **used to** be an elementary school teacher in India. But for the past two years in the U.S., I've been working in a hotel cleaning rooms. I have to work the second shift. I**'m not used to** working nights. I don't like it because I don't see my children very much. When I get home from work, they're asleep. My husband is home in the evening and cooks for them. In India, I **used to** do all the cooking, but now he has to help with household duties. He didn't like it at first, but now he**'s used to** it.

When I started looking for a job, I had to **get used to** a lot of new things. For example, I had to learn to talk about my abilities in an interview. In India, it is considered impolite to say how wonderful you are. But my job counselor told me that I had to **get used to** it because that's what Americans do. Another thing I**'m not used to** is wearing American clothes. In India, I **used to** wear traditional Indian clothes to work. But now I wear a uniform to work. I don't like to dress like this. I prefer traditional Indian clothes, but my job requires a uniform. There's one thing I can't **get used to**: everyone here calls each other by their first names. It's our native custom to use a term of respect with people we don't know.

It has been hard to **get used to** so many new things, but little by little, I'm doing it.

10.13 Used To vs. Be Used To

Used to + base form is different from *be used to* + gerund.

EXAMPLES	EXPLANATION
Rita **used to be** an elementary school teacher. Now she cleans hotel rooms. She **used to wear** traditional Indian clothes. Now she wears a uniform to work. She **used to cook** dinner for her family in India. Now her husband cooks dinner.	*Used to* + base form tells about a past habit or custom. This activity has been discontinued.
Her husband **didn't use to cook** in India.	The negative is *didn't use to* + base form. (Remove the *d* at the end.)
I'm used to working in the day, not at night. Women in India **are used to wearing** traditional clothes. People who studied British English **aren't used to the American pronunciation**.	*Be used to* + gerund or noun means *be accustomed to*. Something is a person's custom and is therefore not difficult to do. The negative is *be + not + used to* + gerund or noun. (Do not remove the *d* of **used to**.)
If you immigrate to the U.S., you have to **get used to many new things**. Children from another country usually **get used to living** in the U.S. easily. But it takes their parents a long time to **get used to a new life**. I **can't get used to** the cold winters here. She **can't get used to** calling people by their first names.	*Get used to* + gerund or noun means *become accustomed to*. For the negative, we usually say *can't get used to*.

Pronunciation Note: We don't pronounce the *d* in *used to*.

EXERCISE 29 **ABOUT YOU** Write four sentences comparing your former behaviors to your behaviors or customs now.

EXAMPLES   I used to live with my family. Now I live with a roommate.

I used to worry a lot. Now I take it easy most of the time.

1. _____
2. _____
3. _____
4. _____

EXERCISE **30**   **ABOUT YOU**   Write sentences comparing the way you used to live in your country or in another city and the way you live now. Read your sentences to the class.

EXAMPLE   *I used to go everywhere by bus. Now I have a car.*

1. _____
2. _____
3. _____
4. _____

EXERCISE **31**   A student wrote about things that are new for her in an American classroom. Fill in the blanks with a gerund.

EXAMPLE   I'm not used to ___taking___ multiple-choice tests. In my native country, we have essay tests.

1. I'm not used to _____ at small desks. In my native country, we sit at large tables.

2. I'm not used to _____ the teacher by his/her first name. In my country, we say "Professor."

3. I'm not used to _____ in a textbook. In my native country, we don't write in the books because we borrow them from the school.

4. I'm not used to _____ jeans to class. In my native country, students wear a uniform.

5. I'm not used to _____ and studying at the same time. Students in my native country don't work. Their parents support them.

6. I'm not used to _____ a lot of money to attend college. In my native country, college is free.

7. I'm not used to _____ when a teacher asks me a question. In my native country, students stand to answer a question.

EXERCISE 32 **ABOUT YOU** Name four things that you had to get used to in the U.S. or in a new town or school. (These things were strange for you when you arrived.)

EXAMPLES I had to get used to ___living in a small apartment.___

I had to get used to ___American pronunciation.___

1. I had to get used to _____
2. I had to get used to _____
3. I had to get used to _____
4. I had to get used to _____

EXERCISE 33 **ABOUT YOU** Answer each question with a complete sentence. Practice *be used to* + gerund or noun.

EXAMPLES What are you used to drinking in the morning?
I'm used to drinking coffee in the morning.
What kind of food are you used to? I'm used to Mexican food.

1. What kind of work are you used to?
2. What kind of relationship are you used to having with coworkers?
3. What kind of food are you used to (eating)?
4. What kind of weather are you used to?
5. What time are you used to getting up?
6. What kinds of clothes are you used to wearing to work or class?
7. What kinds of things are you used to doing every day?
8. What kinds of classroom behaviors are you used to?
9. What kinds of things are you used to doing alone?

EXERCISE 34 Circle the correct words to complete this conversation.

CD 3, TR 24

A: How's your new job?

B: I don't like it at all. I have to work the night shift. I can't get used to (*sleep* / *sleeping*) during the day.
(example)

A: I know. That's hard. I used to (*work* / *working*) the night shift, and I
(1)
hated it. That's why I quit.

B: But the night shift pays more money.

A: I know it does, but I was never home for my children. Now my kids speak more English than Spanish. They used to *(speaking / speak)*
(2)
Spanish well, but now they mix Spanish and English. They play with their American friends all day or watch TV.

B: My kids are the same way. But *(I'm / I)* used
(3)
to it. It doesn't bother me.

A: I can't *(get / be)* used to it. My parents came
(4)
to live with us, and they don't speak much English. So they can't communicate with their grandchildren anymore.

B: My parents used to *(living / live)* with us too. But they went back
(5)
to Mexico. They didn't like the winters here. They couldn't get *(use / used)* to the cold weather.
(6)

A: Do you think Americans are *(used to / use to)* cold weather?
(7)

B: I'm not sure. My coworker was born in the U.S., but she says she hates winter. She *(is used to / used to)* live in Texas, but now she
(8)
lives here in Minnesota.

A: Why did she move here if she hates the cold weather?

B: The company where she used to *(work / working)* closed down
(9)
and she had to find another job. Her cousin helped her find a job here.

A: Before I came to the U.S., I thought everything here would be perfect. I didn't *(use / used)* to *(think / thinking)* about the
(10)   (11)
problems. But I guess life in every country has its problems.

Summary of Lesson 10

Gerunds

EXAMPLES	EXPLANATION
Working all day is hard.	As the subject of the sentence
I don't enjoy **working** as a taxi driver.	After certain verbs
I **go shopping** after work.	In many idiomatic expressions with *go*
I'm worried about **finding** a job.	After prepositions
She found a job by **looking** in the newspaper.	In adverbial phrases

Infinitives

EXAMPLES	EXPLANATION
I need **to find** a new job.	After certain verbs
My boss wants me **to work** overtime.	After an object
I'm ready **to quit**.	After certain adjectives
It's important **to have** some free time. It's impossible for me **to work** 80 hours a week.	After certain impersonal expressions beginning with *it*
I work (in order) **to support** my family.	To show purpose

Gerund or Infinitive—No Difference in Meaning

GERUND	INFINITIVE
I like **working** with computers. I began **working** three months ago.	I like **to work** with computers. I began **to work** three months ago.
Writing a good résumé is important.	It's important **to write** a good résumé.

Gerund or Infinitive—Difference in Meaning

INFINITIVE (PAST HABIT)	GERUND (CUSTOM)
Rita **used to be** a teacher in India. Now she works in a hotel.	She **isn't used to working** the night shift. It's hard for her.
Rita **used to wear** traditional Indian clothes to work. Now she wears a uniform.	Rita studied British English. She had to **get used to hearing** the American pronunciation.

Editing Advice

1. Use a gerund after a preposition.

   using
   He read the whole book without ~~use~~ a dictionary.

2. Use the correct preposition.

   on
   She insisted ~~in~~ driving me home.

3. Use a gerund after certain verbs.

   ing
   I enjoy ~~to~~ walk ^ in the park.

   ping
   He went ~~to~~ shop ^ after work.

4. Use an infinitive after certain verbs.

   to
   I decided ^ buy a new car.

5. Use a gerund, not a base form, as a subject.

   Finding
   ~~Find~~ a good job is important.

6. Don't forget to include *it* for a delayed infinitive subject.

   It's
   ~~Is~~ important to find a good job.

7. Don't use the past form after *to*.

   buy
   I decided to ~~bought~~ a new car.

8. After *want, expect, need, advise,* and *ask,* use an object pronoun, not a subject pronoun, before the infinitive. Don't use *that* as a connector.

   me to
   He wants ~~that I~~ drive.

   us to
   The teacher expects ~~we~~ do the homework.

9. Use *for,* not *to,* when introducing an object after impersonal expressions beginning with *it.* Use the object pronoun after *for.*

   for
   It's important ~~to~~ me to find a job.

   him
   It's necessary for ~~he~~ to be on time.

10. Use *to* + base form, not *for*, to show purpose.

                                  to

       I called the company ~~for~~ make an appointment.

11. Don't put *be* before *used to* for the habitual past.

        I

       ~~I'm~~ used to live in Germany. Now I live in the U.S.

12. Don't use the *-ing* form after *used to* for the habitual past.

                 have

       We used to ~~having~~ a dog, but he died.

13. Don't forget the *d* in *used to*.

              d

       I use to live with my parents. Now I live alone.

Editing Quiz

Some of the shaded words and phrases have mistakes. Find the mistakes and correct them. If the shaded words are correct, write *C*.

                  to   *C*

    I'm planning be a nurse. I'd love to be a doctor, but I don't want be in
     (example)   *(example)*   *(1)*

school for so many years. My mother is a doctor and she wanted I study
                                                        (2)

medicine too. I know that you're never too old to learn something new,
                                              (3)

but I'm 35 years old and start something new at my age is not easy. Study
                            (4)   *(5)*

to become a doctor takes too long. It would take me eight years become
                                                     (6)

a doctor. I went to my college counselor to get advice. My counselor
                                           (7)

recommended entering a nursing program instead. She advised me take
                    (8)   *(9)*

biology and chemistry this semester as well as English and math. It's hard

to me to take so many courses, but I have no choice.
(10)

    In my country, I'm used to work in a nursing home. I enjoyed to help
                           (11)   *(12)*

older people, but I didn't make enough money. When I decided to came
                                                     (13)

to the U.S., I had to think about my future. People say that is not hard
                                                     (14)

to find a job as a nurse in the U.S. It's important for me to be in a profession
  (15)   *(16)*

where I can help people. And I can do that more quickly by going into a
                                                   (17)

nursing program.

Lesson 10 Test/Review

PART **1** **Fill in the blanks in the conversation below. Use a gerund or an infinitive. In some cases, either the gerund or the infinitive is possible. Answers may vary.**

A: Hi, Molly. I haven't seen you in ages. What's going on in your life?

B: I've made many changes. First, I quit __**working**__ in a factory.

(example)

I disliked _____ the same thing every day. And I wasn't

(1)

used to _____ on my feet all day. My boss often wanted me

(2)

_____ overtime on Saturdays. I need _____ with my

(3) *(4)*

children on Saturdays. Sometimes they want me _____

(5)

them to the zoo or to the museum. And I need _____ them

(6)

with their homework too.

A: So what do you plan on _____ ?

(7)

B: I've started _____ to college _____ some general courses.

(8) *(9)*

A: What career are you planning?

B: I'm not sure. I'm interested in _____ with children. Maybe I'll

(10)

become a teacher's aide. I've also thought about _____ in a day

(11)

care center. I care about _____ people.

(12)

A: Yes, it's wonderful _____ other people, especially children. It's

(13)

important _____ a job that you like. So you're starting a whole

(14)

new career.

B: It's not new, really. Before I came to the U.S., I used _____

(15)

a kindergarten teacher in my country. But my English wasn't

so good when I came here, so I found a job in a factory. I look

forward to _____ to my former profession or doing

(16)

something similar.

A: How did you learn English so fast?

(continued)

B: By _____ with people at work, by _____ TV, and by
         (17)   (18)
_____ the newspaper. It hasn't been easy for me _____
   (19)   (20)
American English. I studied British English in my country, but

here I have to get used to _____ things like "gonna" and
                              (21)

"wanna." At first I didn't understand Americans, but now I'm

used to their pronunciation. I've had to make a lot of changes.

A: You should be proud of _____ so many changes in your life
                                  (22)

so quickly.

B: I am.

A: Let's get together some time and talk some more.

B: I'd love to. I love to dance. Maybe we can go _____ together
                                                         (23)

sometime.

A: That would be great. And I love _____. Maybe we can go
                                          (24)

shopping together sometime.

PART 2   **Fill in the blanks with the correct preposition. If no preposition is
             necessary, write X in the blank.**

EXAMPLES   I believe _____ doing my best.
                            in

               Not _____ knowing English well makes it hard to find a job.
                       X

   1. She dreams _____ becoming an engineer.

   2. Are you good _____ working with people?

   3. I'm not worried _____ finding a job.

   4. When he's not working, he likes to go _____ fishing.

   5. You can prepare for an interview _____ practicing with a friend.

   6. A nurse is responsible _____ improving a patient's health.

   7. Do you mind _____ working in a restaurant?

   8. She went to a job counselor _____ get advice.

   9. It's important _____ him to finish college.

   10. I want you _____ help me write a résumé.

Expansion

❶ **If you have a job, write a list of five things you enjoy and don't enjoy about your job. If you don't have a job, you can write about what you enjoy and don't enjoy about this school or class. Share your answers with the class.**

❷ **Compare the work environment in the U.S. to the work environment in another country. Discuss your answers in a small group or with the entire class. (If you have no experience with American jobs, ask an American to fill in his/her opinions about the U.S.)**

	The U.S.	Another Country
1. Coworkers are friendly with each other at the job.		
2. Coworkers get together after work to socialize.		
3. Arriving on time for the job is very important.		
4. The boss is friendly with the employees.		
5. The employees are very serious about their jobs.		
6. The employees use the telephone for personal use.		
7. Everyone wears formal clothes.		
8. Employees get long lunch breaks.		
9. Employees get long vacations.		
10. Employees call the company if they are sick and can't work on a particular day.		
11. Employees are paid in cash.		
12. Employees often take work home.		

❸ **Find a partner. Pretend that one of you is the manager of a company and the other one is looking for a job in that company. First decide what kind of company it is. Then write the manager's questions and the applicant's answers. Perform your interview in front of the class.**

Talk
About It

1 Talk about your experiences in looking for a job in the U.S.

2 Talk about the environment where you work.

3 Talk about some professions that interest you.

4 Talk about some professions that you think are terrible.

Write
About It

1 Write your résumé and a cover letter.

2 Write about a job you wouldn't want to have. Tell why.

3 Write about a profession you would like to have. Tell why.

4 Write about your current job or a job you had in the past. Tell what you like(d) or don't (didn't) like about this job.

My Last Job

I used to work as a server in a restaurant. I hated this job for several reasons. First, my boss expected me to be on my feet all day even when the restaurant was empty. Also, I didn't like the customers. I always tried to be nice to them, but some of them weren't nice to me . . .

 For more practice using grammar in context, please visit our Web site.

Grammar
Adjective Clauses

Context
**Making Connections—
Old Friends and New**

11.1 Adjective Clauses—An Overview

An adjective is a word that describes a noun. An adjective clause is a group of words (with a subject and a verb) that describes a noun. Compare adjectives (ADJ) and adjective clauses (AC) below.

EXAMPLES	EXPLANATION
ADJ: Do you know your **new** neighbors? **AC:** Do you know the people **who live next door to you**?	An adjective (ADJ) precedes a noun.
ADJ: This is an **interesting** book. **AC:** This is a book **that has pictures of the high school graduates**.	An adjective clause (AC) follows a noun.
ADJ: I attended an **old** high school. **AC:** The high school **that I attended** was built in 1920.	Relative pronouns, such as *who* and *that*, introduce an adjective clause.

Finding Old Friends

Before
You Read

1. Do you keep in touch with old friends from your previous schools?

2. Have you ever thought about contacting someone you haven't seen in years?

CD 4, TR 01

Read the following magazine article. Pay special attention to adjective clauses.

Americans move numerous times during their lives. As a result, they often lose touch with old friends. Usually, during their twenties and thirties, people are too busy building their careers and starting their families to think much about the past. But as people get older, they often start to wonder about the best friend **they had in high school**, the soldier **with whom they served in the military**, the person **who lived next door** when they were growing up, or their high school sweetheart. Many people want to connect with the past.

Before the Internet, finding a lost love or an old friend required searching through old phone books in libraries in different cities, hard work, and a lot of luck. It was especially hard to find married women **who changed their names**.

Now with the Internet, old friends can sometimes find each other in seconds. Several Web sites have emerged to meet people's growing desire to make connections with former classmates. There are Web sites **that list the students in high schools and colleges in the U.S.** People **who went to high school in the U.S.** can list themselves according to the school **they attended** and the year **they graduated**. A man might go to these Web sites looking for the guys **he played football with** or a long-lost friend—and find the name of a first love **whom he hasn't seen in years**.

One Web site, Classmates.com, claims that more than 40 million Americans have listed themselves on their site. Married women **who have changed their names** list themselves by their maiden names so that others can recognize them easily.

High School Yearbook

Another way **that people make connections with old classmates** is through reunions. Some high school graduating classes meet every ten years. They usually have dinner, remember the time **when they were young,** and exchange information about what they are doing today. They sometimes bring their high school yearbooks, **which have pictures of the graduates and other school memories**.

Some classes have their reunions in the schools **where they first met.** Others have their reunions in a nice restaurant. There are Web sites **that specialize in helping people find their former classmates and plan reunions**.

In America's highly mobile society, it takes some effort to connect with old friends. Looking back at fond memories, renewing old friendships, making new friends, and even starting a new romance with an old love can be the reward for a little work on the Internet.

EXERCISE 1 **Tell if the statement is true or false based on the reading on pages 358–359. Write *T* or *F*.**

EXAMPLE   People who attend reunions meet their old classmates.   T

1. A yearbook is a book that has the diplomas of the graduates.
2. Classmates.com is a Web site that has lists of students from various high schools in the U.S.
3. Americans move a lot and often lose touch with the friends that they had in high school.
4. Women who get married list their maiden names on Classmates.com.
5. People who graduate from high school have to attend their reunions.
6. There are several Web sites that help people make connections with old friends.

EXERCISE 2 **Underline the adjective clauses in the sentences in Exercise 1.**

EXAMPLE   People <u>who attend reunions</u> meet their old classmates.

11.2 Relative Pronoun as Subject

The relative pronouns *who*, *that*, and *which* can be the subject of the adjective clause. Use *who* or *that* for people. Use *that* or *which* for things.

Subject
I found a Web site. *The Web site* lists people by high school.
I found a Web site **that** lists people by high school. **which**

Women . . . . .often change their last names.
Subject
Women get married.
who
Women **that** get married often change their last names.

Language Notes:
1. *That* is considered more correct than *which*.
2. A present tense verb in the adjective clause must agree in number with its subject.
   A woman who **gets** married usually changes her name.
   Women who **get** married usually change their names.

EXERCISE 3   Fill in the blanks with *who* for people and *that* for objects + the correct form of the verb in parentheses ( ).

EXAMPLE   A yearbook has photos _____*that show*_____ the activities of the high school.
                                            (show)

1. He has a yearbook _____ pictures of all his classmates.
                              (have)

2. People _____ to a reunion exchange information
                (go)

   about their lives.

3. Classmates.com is a Web site _____ people make
                                        (help)

   connections with old friends.

4. There are Web sites _____ in helping people
                            (specialize)

   plan a reunion.

5. People _____ a reunion contact former classmates.
              (plan)

EXERCISE 4   Fill in the blanks with *who* or *that* + the correct form of the verb in parentheses ( ). Then complete the statement. Answers will vary.

EXAMPLE   People _____*who work*_____ hard *are often successful.*
                            (work)

1. People _____ regularly _____
                (exercise)

2. A person _____ a cell phone while
                  (use)

   driving _____

3. Students _____ absent a lot _____
                 (be)

4. Schools _____ computers _____
                (not/have)

5. A computer _____ more than five years old
                     (be)

   _____

6. People _____ digital cameras _____
                (have)

7. Colleges _____ evening classes _____
                  (have)

8. A college _____ a day-care center _____
                   (have)

9. Students _____ a job _____
                 (have)

EXERCISE 5   **Complete each statement with an adjective clause. Answers will vary.**

EXAMPLE   I know some women ___who OR that don't want to get married___.

1. People _____ can make a lot of friends.

2. Men _____ have a busy social life.

3. I like people _____.

4. I don't like people _____.

5. Students like a teacher _____.

6. People _____ are very fortunate.

7. People _____ aren't usually successful.

8. Parents _____ are good.

9. A college _____ is good for foreign students.

10. People _____ have a hard life.

11.3 Relative Pronoun as Object

The relative pronouns *who(m)*, *that*, and *which* can be the object of the adjective clause.

Object
She attended *the high school*.

The high school . . . . is in New York City.
           which
The high school **that** she attended is in New York City.
         Ø

Object
I knew *a friend* in high school.

A friend . . . . sent me an e-mail.
    who(m)
A friend **that** I knew in high school sent me an e-mail.
    Ø

Language Notes:
1. The relative pronoun is usually omitted in conversation when it is the object of the adjective clause.
        The high school she attended is in New York City.
2. *Whom* is considered more correct or more formal than *who* when used as the object of the adjective clause. However, as seen in the above note, the relative pronoun is usually omitted altogether in conversation.
        Formal: A friend *whom* I knew in high school sent me an e-mail.
        Informal: A friend I knew in high school sent me an e-mail.

EXERCISE 6 **In each sentence below, underline the adjective clause.**

EXAMPLE I've lost touch with some of the friends <u>I had in high school</u>.

1. The high school I attended is in another city.
2. The teachers I had in high school are all old now.
3. We didn't have to buy the textbooks we used in high school.
4. She married a man she met in college.
5. The friends I've made in this country don't know much about my country.

EXERCISE 7 **A mother (M) is talking to her teenage daughter (D). Fill in the blanks to complete the conversation. Answers may vary.**

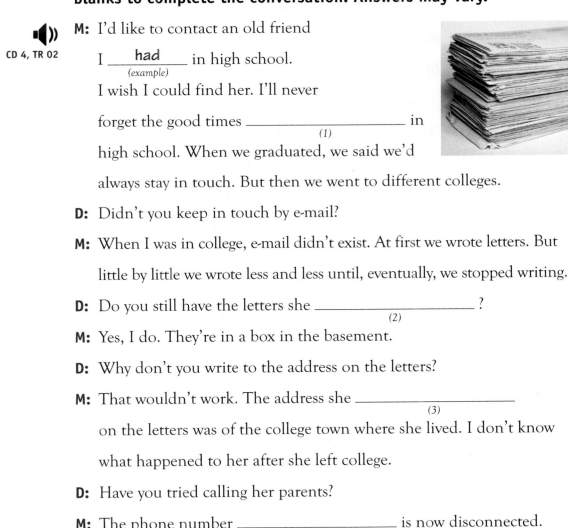

CD 4, TR 02

M: I'd like to contact an old friend

I ___**had**___ in high school.
   (example)
I wish I could find her. I'll never

forget the good times _____ in
                              (1)
high school. When we graduated, we said we'd

always stay in touch. But then we went to different colleges.

D: Didn't you keep in touch by e-mail?

M: When I was in college, e-mail didn't exist. At first we wrote letters. But

little by little we wrote less and less until, eventually, we stopped writing.

D: Do you still have the letters she _____ ?
                                           (2)
M: Yes, I do. They're in a box in the basement.

D: Why don't you write to the address on the letters?

M: That wouldn't work. The address she _____
                                             (3)
on the letters was of the college town where she lived. I don't know

what happened to her after she left college.

D: Have you tried calling her parents?

M: The phone number _____ is now disconnected.
                         (4)
Maybe her parents have died.

D: Have you looked on Classmates.com?

M: What's that?

(continued)

D: It's a Web site that _____ lists of people. The lists are
(5)

categorized by the high school you _____ and the
(6)

dates you _____ there.
(7)

M: Is everyone in my high school class on the list?

D: Unfortunately, no. Only the people _____ add their
(8)

names are on the list.

M: But my friend probably got married. I don't know the name of the

man _____ married.
(9)

D: That's not a problem. You can search for her by her maiden name.

M: Will this Web site give me her address and phone number?

D: No. But for a fee, you can send her an e-mail through the Web site. Then

if she wants to contact you, she can give you her personal information.

M: She'll probably think I'm crazy for contacting her almost 25 years later.

D: I'm sure she'll be happy to receive communication from a good friend

_____ hasn't seen in years. When I graduate
(10)

from high school, I'm never going to lose contact with the

friends _____ made. We'll always stay in touch.
(11)

M: That's what you think. But as time passes and your lives become more

complicated, you may lose touch.

D: But today we have e-mail.

M: Well, e-mail is a help. Even so, the direction you _____
(12)

in life is different from the direction your friends choose.

EXERCISE 8 **Fill in the blanks with appropriate words to complete the
conversation. Answers may vary.**

CD 4, TR 03

A: I'm lonely. I have a lot of friends in my native country, but I don't

have enough friends here. The friends ___**I have there**___ send me
(example)

e-mail all the time, but that's not enough. I need to make new friends here.

B: Haven't you met any people here?

A: Of course. But the people _____ here don't have my
(1)

interests.

B: What are you interested in?

A: I like reading, meditating, going for quiet walks. Americans seem to like parties, TV, sports, movies, going to restaurants.

B: You're never going to meet people with the interests
_____. Your interests don't include other people.
      (2)
You should find some interests _____ other people, like
      (3)
tennis or dancing, to mention just a few.

A: The activities _____ cost money, and I don't have a lot
      (4)
of money.

B: There are many parks in this city _____ free tennis courts.
      (5)
If you like to dance, I know of a park district near here
_____ free dance classes. In fact, there are a lot of
      (6)
things _____ or very low cost in this city. I can give you a
      (7)
list of free activities, if you want.

A: Thanks. I'd love to have the list. Thanks for all the suggestions
_____.
      (8)

B: I'd be happy to give you more, but I don't have time now. Tomorrow
I'll e-mail you a list of activities from the parks in this city. I'm sure
you'll find something _____ on that list.
      (9)

A: Thanks.

EXERCISE 9 **We often give a definition with an adjective clause. Work with a partner to give a definition of the following words by using an adjective clause.**

EXAMPLES twins
Twins are brothers or sisters who are born at the same time.

an answering machine
An answering machine is a device that takes phone messages.

1. a babysitter

2. an immigrant

3. an adjective

4. a verb

5. a fax machine

6. a dictionary

7. a computer mouse

8. a coupon

11.4 *Where* and *When*

EXAMPLES	EXPLANATION
Some classmates have their reunion in the school **where they first met.** There are Web sites **where you can find lists of high schools and their students.** She attended the University of Washington, **where she met her best friend.**	*Where* means "in that place." *Where* cannot be omitted.
Do you remember the time **(when) you were in high school?** High school was a time **(when) I had many good friends and few responsibilities.** In 1998, **when I graduated from high school**, my best friend's family moved to another state.	*When* means "at that time." *When* can sometimes be omitted.

Punctuation Notes:
1. An adjective clause is sometimes separated from the sentence with a comma. This is true when the person or thing in the main clause is unique.

Compare:
> I visited a Web site **where** I found the names of my classmates. (No comma)
> I visited Classmates.com, **where** I found the names of my classmates. (Comma: Classmates.com is a unique Web site.)
> I remember the year **when** I graduated from high school. (No comma)
> In 1998, **when** she graduated from high school, she got married. (Comma: 1998 is a unique year.)

2. Only *when* without a comma can be omitted.
> I remember the year I graduated from high school.

EXERCISE **This is a conversation between a son (S) and his dad (D). Fill in the blanks with *where* or *when* to complete this conversation.**

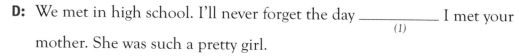

CD 4, TR 04

S: How did you meet Mom? Do you remember the place ___where___
(example)
you met?

D: We met in high school. I'll never forget the day _____ I met your
(1)
mother. She was such a pretty girl.

S: Did you go to the same school?

D: Yes. We were in a typing class together. She was sitting at the typewriter next to mine.

S: Dad, what's a typewriter?

D: There was a time _____ we didn't have computers. We had
(2)

to type our papers on typewriters.

S: Did you start dating right away?

D: No. We were friends. There was a time _____ people were
(3)

friends before they started dating. There was a soda shop near

school _____ we used to meet.
(4)

S: What's a soda shop, Dad?

D: It's a store _____ you could buy milk shakes, sodas, and
(5)

hamburgers. We used to sit there after school drinking one soda with

two straws.

S: That doesn't seem too romantic to me.

D: But it was.

S: So did you get married as soon as you graduated from high school?

D: No. I graduated from high school at a time _____ there was
(6)

a war going on in this country. Mom went to college and I went into the

army. We wrote letters during that time. When I got out of the army, I

started college. So we got married about seven years after we met.

11.5 Formal vs. Informal

EXAMPLES	EXPLANATION
Informal: I lost touch with the friends I went to high school **with**. **Formal:** I lost touch with the friends **with whom** I went to high school.	Informally, most native speakers put the preposition at the end of the adjective clause. The relative pronoun is usually omitted.
Informal: I saved the yearbook my friends wrote **in**. **Formal:** I saved the yearbook **in which** my friends wrote.	In very formal English, the preposition comes before the relative pronoun, and only *whom* and *which* may be used. *Who* and *that* are not used directly after a preposition.

EXAMPLE   What is the name of the high school you graduated from?

What is the name of the high school from which you graduated?

1. He found his friend that he served in the military with.

_____

2. I can't find the friend I was looking for.

_____

3. The high school she graduated from was torn down.

_____

4. Do you remember the teacher I was talking about?

_____

5. In high school, the activities I was interested in were baseball and band.

_____

Social Networking in the Twenty-First Century

Before
You Read

1. Where or how do you meet new people?

2. Do you use social networking Web sites? Which ones?

CD 4, TR 05

Read the following magazine article. Pay special attention to adjective clauses beginning with _whose_.

The method of social networking has changed in the twenty-first century, thanks to the Internet. Mark Zuckerman,  the creator of one popular site, Facebook, started his network in 2004, when he was a student at Harvard University. He realized that students, **whose** lives are very busy, wanted to be able to find out about their friends' thoughts and activities. By 2007, Facebook had 70 million users. Other social networking sites, like Friendster and MySpace, also became popular all over the world.
When asked "Why did you join this site?", here is how some people responded:

• I'm interested in politics, and it's a good way to find people **whose** interests are the same as mine.

- I can share photos with my friends and make comments on their photos.
- I can see what friends we have in common.
- I can hear about events from my friends.
- I can share my favorite links with my friends.

Who are the members of these social networking sites? At first, they were mostly teenagers and college students. Soon parents **whose** kids were hooked on social networking started joining too.

Another way to bring together people **whose** interests are the same is through a Web site called Meetup.com. Unlike online social networking, **whose** members learn about each other's activities on a Web site, Meetup members get notices about events online but actually get together in coffeehouses, restaurants, parks, etc. A big city like New York has over 4,000 Meetup groups per week, ranging from chess players to book lovers, bicyclists, and French speakers.

The Internet brings people together in creative ways.

11.6 *Whose* + Noun

Whose is the possessive form of *who*. It substitutes for *his*, *her*, *its*, *their*, or the possessive form of the noun.

I want to meet people.
Their interests are the same as mine.
I want to meet people **whose** interests are the same as mine.
Students . . . . like to communicate with their friends online.
Their lives are busy.
Students **whose** lives are busy like to communicate with their friends online.

Language Note: Use *who* to substitute for a person. Use *whose* for possession or relationship.

Compare:
   I want to meet people **who** are interested in sports.
   I want to meet people **whose** interests are the same as mine.

Punctuation Note: An adjective clause is sometimes separated from the sentence with a comma. This is true when the person or thing in the main clause is unique.
   I go to a meetup whose members are interested in sports.
   Facebook, whose members pay nothing, is a popular social networking site.
   (Facebook is unique.)

EXERCISE 12 Fill in the blanks with one of the words from the box below.

EXAMPLE Do you want to meet people whose _interests_ are the same as yours?

schoolwork	kids	friends
photos	interests ✓	members

1. Students whose _____ keeps them busy want a way to know about their friends.

2. Meetup.com, whose _____ get together, is a good way to meet people with similar interests.

3. Parents whose _____ use Facebook are starting to become interested in it too.

4. I like to see the profiles of friends whose _____ are on the site. If they don't post their pictures, I'm not interested.

5. People whose _____ are on Facebook often get an invitation to join.

EXERCISE 13 **ABOUT YOU** Fill in the blanks.

EXAMPLE I would like to own a car that _has enough room for my large family._

1. My mother is/was a woman who _____

2. My city is a place where _____

3. My childhood was a time when _____

4. My favorite kind of book is one that _____

5. A great teacher is a person who _____

6. I have a friend whose _____

7. I have a computer that _____

8. I like to shop at a time when _____

9. I don't like people who _____

EXERCISE 14 Some people were asked what kind of friends they'd like to meet. Fill in the blanks with a response, using the words in parentheses ( ).

EXAMPLE I'd like to meet people _whose values are the same as mine._

(Their values are the same as mine.)

1. I'd like to find a friend _____

(I can trust him.)

2. I don't want to be with students _____

(They don't take school seriously.)

3. I want to meet people _____

(They like to play soccer.)

4. I joined a French meetup _____

(Its members speak French very well.)

5. We meet in a coffee shop _____

(It isn't crowded in the morning.)

6. I go to a book club meetup _____

(It meets near my house.)

7. My math group is a club _____

(I found it on Meetup.com.)

EXERCISE 15 **Fill in the blanks with appropriate words to complete the conversation. Answers may vary.**

CD 4, TR 06

A: I'm getting married in two months.

B: Congratulations. Are you marrying the woman ____**you met**____
  (example)

at Mark's party last year?

A: Oh, no. I broke up with that woman a long time ago. I'm going to

marry a woman _____ online about ten months ago.
  (1)

B: What's your fiancée's name? Do I know her?

A: Sarah Liston.

B: I know someone whose _____ is Liston.
  (2)

I wonder if they're from the same family.

A: I doubt it. Sarah comes from Canada.

B: Where are you going to live after you get married? Here or in Canada?

A: We're going to live here. Sarah's just finishing college and doesn't

have a job yet. This is the place _____ I have a good job,
  (3)

so we decided to live here.

B: Where are you going to get married?

(continued)

A: At my parents' friends' house. They have a very big house and garden. The wedding's going to be in the garden.

B: My wife and I made plans to get married outside too, but we had to change our plans because it rained that day.

A: That's OK. The woman _____ is more important
(4)
than the place _____ we get married. And the
(5)
life _____ together is more important than the
(6)
wedding day.

B: You're right about that!

EXERCISE 16 **Use the words in parentheses ( ) to form an adjective clause. Then read the sentences and tell if you agree or disagree. Give your reasons.**

EXAMPLE   A good friend is a person ___**(whom) I can trust**___.
(I can trust her.)

1. A good friend is a person _____ almost every day.
(I see him.)

2. A good friend is a person _____.
(She would lend me money.)

3. A good friend is a person _____.
(He knows everything about me.)

4. A person _____ cannot be my friend.
(He has different political opinions.)

5. A person _____ cannot be my good friend.
(She doesn't speak my native language.)

6. A person _____ cannot be my good friend.
(His religious beliefs are different from mine.)

7. A person _____ cannot be a good friend.
(She lives far away.)

8. It's important to have friends _____.
(Their interests are the same as mine.)

9. This school is a place _____.
(I can make many new friends easily at this school.)

10. Childhood is the only time in one's life _____

_____.
(It is easy to make friends at this time.)

Summary of Lesson 11

Adjective Clauses

1. Pronoun as Subject

    She has a friend **who lives in Alaska.**
    The man **that arrived late** took a seat in the back.

2. Pronoun as Object

    I have some friends **(who/whom/that) I met online.**
    The book **(which/that) I'm reading** is very exciting.

3. Pronoun as Object of Preposition

    Formal: The person **about whom I'm talking** is my cousin.
    Informal: The person **(who) I'm talking about** is my cousin.

    Formal: The club **of which I am a member** meets at the community center.
    Informal: The club **(that) I am a member of** meets at the community center.

4. *Whose* + Noun

    I have a friend **whose brother lives in Japan.**
    The students **whose last names begin with A or B** can register on Friday afternoon.

5. *Where*

    He moved to New Jersey, **where he found a job.**
    The apartment building **where he lives** has a lot of immigrant families.

6. *When*

    She came to the U.S. at a time **when she was young enough to learn English easily.**
    She came to the U.S. in 1995, **when there was a war going on in her country.**

Editing Advice

1. Use *who*, *that*, or *which* to introduce an adjective clause. Don't use *what*.

    I know a woman ~~what~~ has ten cats.
    who

2. If the relative pronoun is the subject, don't omit it.

    I know a man has visited every state in the U.S.
    who

3. Use *whose* to substitute for a possessive form.

> *whose*
> I live next door to a couple ~~their~~ children make a lot of noise.

4. If the relative pronoun is used as the object, don't put an object after the verb of the adjective clause.

> I had to pay for the library book that I lost ~~it~~.

5. Don't use *which* for people.

> *who*
> The man ~~which~~ bought my car paid me by check.

6. Use subject-verb agreement in all clauses.

> s
> I have a friend who live in Madrid.

> People who talk~~s~~ too much bother me.

7. Don't use an adjective clause when a simple adjective is enough.

> *I don't like long movies.*
> ~~I don't like movies that are long.~~

8. Put a noun before an adjective clause.

> *A student who*
> ~~Who~~ needs help should ask the teacher.

9. Use *where*, not *that*, to mean "in a place."

> *where*
> The store ~~that~~ I buy my textbooks is having a sale this week.

10. Use *whom* and *which*, not *who* and *that*, if the preposition precedes the relative pronoun.

> *which*
> She would never want to go back to the country from ~~that~~ she came.

> *whom*
> I don't know the person about ~~who~~ you are talking.

11. Use the correct word order in an adjective clause (subject before verb).

> *my father caught*
> The fish that ~~caught my father~~ was very big.

12. Don't confuse *whose* (possessive form) and *who's* (*who is*).

> *who's*
> A woman ~~whose~~ in my math class is helping me study for the test.

Editing Quiz

Some of the shaded words and phrases have mistakes. Find the mistakes and correct them. If the shaded words are correct, write C.

C

I would like to find one of the friends that I had in college. I found a Web site
(example)

where

~~that~~ I can look for old friends. My friend, whose name is Linda Gast,
(example) (1)

got married shortly after we graduated. The man which she married is Bart
(2)

Reed. I tried using the names "Linda Gast" and "Linda Reed" but I had no

luck. I found a woman with who she shared a room in college, and she
(3)

gave me a phone number. The phone number that gave me her roommate
(4) (5)

is not in service anymore. I called a man what used to be her neighbor, but
(6)

he said that she moved away a long time ago. The last reunion that I
(7)

attended it was four years ago, but she wasn't there. The people were our
(8) (9)

friends in high school didn't know anything about her. I looked in the

phone book and found some people their name is the same as hers, but
(10)

they weren't the right people. I went back to the high school that we were
(11)

students, but they had no information about her. Because of the Internet,

now is a time when it's easier than ever to find people. But my search, which
(12) (13)

have taken me almost five years, has produced no result. Recently I met
(14)

someone whose a friend of her brother, and he told me that Linda's now
(15)

living in South America. He's going to try to find Linda's current address.

Looking for Linda is a job that is hard, but I'm determined to find her.
(16)

Who tries hard enough usually succeeds.
(17)

Lesson 11 Test/Review

PART 1 Fill in the blanks with *who, whom, that, which, whose, where, when* or *Ø*. In some cases, more than one answer is possible.

1. I'm still friends with the people _____ I met in elementary school.
2. Childhood is the time _____ it's easiest to make friends.
3. The elementary school _____ I attended is in Poland.
4. I'm still in contact with some of the teachers _____ I admired a lot.
5. There are some teachers _____ names I've forgotten.
6. The university is the place _____ my father met my mother.
7. Now I use social networking sites _____ allow me to exchange information with my friends.
8. I don't know if they're real friends. For me, a friend is a person _____ I can really trust.

PART 2 Fill in the blanks to complete the adjective clause. Answers may vary.

EXAMPLE **A:** You lost a glove. Is this yours?

B: No. The glove _____(that) I lost_____ is brown.

1. **A:** My neighbor's children make a lot of noise.

   B: That's too bad. I don't like to have neighbors _____

   _____.

2. **A:** I have a new cat. Do you want to see him?

   B: What happened to the other cat _____?

   A: She died last month.

3. **A:** Do you speak French?

   B: Yes, I do. Why?

   A: The teacher is looking for a student _____ to help her translate a letter.

4. **A:** Did you meet your boyfriend on an Internet dating site?

   B: No. I didn't like any of the guys _____ on the Internet.

5. **A:** Does your last name begin with A?

   B: Yes, it does. Why?

   A: Registration is by alphabetical order. Students _____ _____ can register after 2 P.M. today.

6. **A:** Did you go to your last high school reunion?

   B: No. I was out of town on the day _____.

   A: Do you usually go to your reunions?

   B: Yes. I love to keep in touch with the people _____.

7. **A:** Are you planning to marry Charles?

   B: No. He lives with his mother. I want to marry a man _____ lives far away.

Expansion

Classroom Activities

❶ Write a short definition or description of an object or a person. Read your definition to a small group. The others will try to guess what it is. Continue to add to your definition until someone guesses it.

EXAMPLE   It's an animal that lives in the water.
Is it a fish?
No, it isn't. It's an animal that needs to come up for air.
Is it a dolphin?
Yes, it is.

❷ Write a word from your native language that has no English translation. It might be the name of a food or a traditional costume. Define the word. Read your definition to a small group or to a partner.

EXAMPLE   A *sari* is a typical Indian dress for women. It is made of a cloth that a woman wraps around her. She wraps one end around her waist. She puts the other end over her shoulder.

❸ Bring to class something typical from your country. Demonstrate how to use it.

EXAMPLE   a samovar
This is a pot that we use in Russia to make tea.

About It

1 Do you think the Internet is a good way to network with friends? Why or why not?

2 How do people in your native culture usually make new friends?

3 What kind of person is a good friend?

4 In your native culture, do people usually keep in touch with the friends they made in school?

5 Are there class reunions in your native country?

Write

About It

1 Write a short composition describing your best friend from your school days.

2 Write a short composition describing the different ways to make new friends.

3 If you use a social networking Web site, write about your experience with it.

Social Networking

Since I started to do social networking online, I've been able to exchange a lot of information with my friends. I always read the short posts that they put on their page every day. Because we're so busy, we often can't find any time when we can get together . . .

 For more practice using grammar in context, please visit our Web site.

Grammar
Superlatives

Comparatives

Context
Sports and Athletes

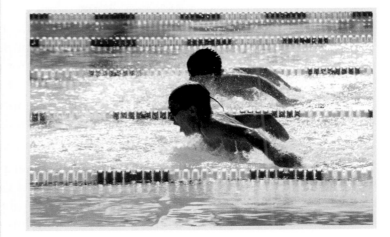

12.1 Superlatives and Comparatives—An Overview

EXAMPLES	EXPLANATION
Baseball and football are **the most popular** sports in the U.S. Jack is **the tallest player** on the basketball team.	We use the superlative form to point out the number one item or items in a group of three or more.
Baseball is **more popular than** soccer in the U.S. Basketball players are **taller than** baseball players.	We use the comparative form to compare two items or groups of items.
He is **as tall as** a basketball player. Soccer is not **as popular as** baseball in the U.S. Soccer players are not **the same height as** basketball players.	We can show equality or inequality of two items or groups of items.

Golf and Tiger Woods

Before
You Read

1. Do you like sports? Which are your favorites?

2. Who are your favorite athletes?

CD 4, TR 07

Read the following Web article. Pay special attention to superlative forms.

http://tigerwoods*golf.com

Golf is the only sport where the player with **the lowest** score wins. The player who puts the ball in the hole with **the fewest** tries (strokes)  is the winner. Golf originally comes from Scotland, where you can still find **the earliest** golf course. Until the beginning of the twentieth century, golf was mainly popular in Scotland and England. Golf is not **the most popular sport** in the U.S., but in recent years the U.S. has produced **the greatest** quantity of leading professional golfers. One of **the most remarkable** players is Tiger Woods.

Tiger Woods was born in 1975 in California. Before he could walk or talk, he loved to watch his father play golf. At age two, he began to play golf with his father—and soon became a better golfer than his father. When Woods was in high school in California, he became **the youngest** person in the U.S. to win the Junior Amateur Championship. At age 19, he became **the youngest** winner of the U.S. Amateur Championship. In 1996, at the age of 21, he became a professional golfer.

Today Woods is one of **the most successful** golfers of all time. He is the only person to be named *Sports Illustrated*'s Sportsman of the Year more than once (in 1996 and 2000).

In 2007, he was **the highest**-paid professional athlete, earning approximately $122 million from winnings and endorsements.[1]

Woods's father died in 2006. Woods wrote on his Web site at the time, "My dad was my **best** friend and **greatest** role model, and I will miss him."

12.2 The Superlative Form

We use the superlative form to point out the number one item of a group of three or more.

EXAMPLES	EXPLANATION
Woods was **the youngest** winner. He worked **the hardest**.	Form: short adjective + *-est* short adverb + *-est*
Golf is not **the most popular** sport in the U.S. Woods learned golf **the most effortlessly** of anyone in his family.	Form: *the most* + longer adjective *the most* + *-ly* adverb
Woods is **one of the most successful** golfer**s**. He is **one of the most remarkable** athlete**s**.	We often say "one of the" before a superlative form. The noun that follows is plural.
In golf, the winner uses **the least** number of strokes. Woods said, "My dad was my **best** friend."	Some superlatives are irregular. See Section 12.3 for more information about irregular forms.
Woods is one of the best golfers **of all time**. Soccer is the most popular sport **in the world**.	We often put a prepositional phrase after a superlative phrase: *in the world, of all time, in the U.S.*, etc.
Woods is one of the best golfers **who has ever lived**. Who is the best athlete **you have ever seen**?	An adjective clause with *ever* and the present perfect tense often completes a superlative statement.

Language Note: Use *the* before a superlative form. Omit *the* if there is a possessive form before the superlative form.
   Woods is one of **the best** golfers. His father was **his best** friend. (not *his the* best friend)

[1]When a famous person makes an *endorsement*, he says that he likes a certain product. He gets paid for saying this.

EXERCISE **1** **Tell if the statement is true (*T*) or false (*F*). Underline the superlative forms.**

EXAMPLE   The <u>oldest</u> golf course is in the U.S.   F

1. In golf, the player with the lowest score wins.
2. Golf is the most popular sport in the U.S.
3. Tiger Woods is one of the best golfers.
4. Tiger's father was his best friend.
5. Tiger's father was one of the best golfers in the world.
6. Tiger Woods is one of the richest athletes.

12.3 Comparative and Superlative Forms of Adjectives and Adverbs

	SIMPLE	COMPARATIVE	SUPERLATIVE
One-syllable adjectives and adverbs*	tall fast	taller faster	the tallest the fastest
Two-syllable adjectives that end in *y*	easy happy	easier happier	the easiest the happiest
Other two-syllable adjectives	frequent active	more frequent more active	the most frequent the most active
Some two-syllable adjectives have two forms.**	simple common	simpler more simple commoner more common	the simplest the most simple the commonest the most common
Adjectives with three or more syllables	important difficult	more important more difficult	the most important the most difficult
-*ly* adverbs	quickly brightly	more quickly more brightly	the most quickly the most brightly
Irregular adjectives and adverbs	good/well bad/badly far little a lot	better worse farther less more	the best the worst the farthest the least the most

Language Notes:

1.*Exceptions to one-syllable adjectives:

    bored   more bored   the most bored
    tired   more tired   the most tired

2.**Other two-syllable adjectives that have two forms:
    handsome, quiet, gentle, narrow, clever, friendly, angry, polite, stupid

Spelling Rules for Short Adjectives and Adverbs

RULE	SIMPLE	COMPARATIVE	SUPERLATIVE
Add -er and -est to short adjectives and adverbs.	tall fast	taller faster	tallest fastest
For adjectives that end in e, add -r and -st.	nice late	nicer later	nicest latest
For adjectives that end in y, change y to i and add -er and -est.	easy happy	easier happier	easiest happiest
For words ending in consonant-vowel-consonant, double the final consonant, then add -er and -est. **Exception:** Do not double final w. new—newer—newest	big sad	bigger sadder	biggest saddest

EXERCISE **2** **Give the comparative and superlative forms of each word.**

EXAMPLES fat   _____fatter_____   _____the fattest_____

important   _____more important_____   _____the most important_____

1. interesting   _____   _____

2. young   _____   _____

3. beautiful   _____   _____

4. good   _____   _____

5. responsible   _____   _____

6. thin   _____   _____

7. carefully   _____   _____

8. pretty   _____   _____

9. bad   _____   _____

10. famous   _____   _____

11. lucky   _____   _____

12. simple   _____   _____

13. high   _____   _____

14. delicious   _____   _____

15. far   _____   _____

16. foolishly   _____   _____

EXERCISE 3 **Write the superlative form of the word in parentheses ( ).**

EXAMPLE Football is one of ___the most dangerous___ sports.
(dangerous)

1. Michael Phelps is _____ swimmer in the world.
(fast)

2. Training for the Olympics is one of _____ things
(difficult)
for an athlete.

3. Soccer is _____ sport in the world.
(popular)

4. Sumo wrestlers are _____ athletes.
(fat)

5. Michael Jordan was _____ basketball player in the
(good)
world.

6. Swimming and gymnastics are _____ events during
(watched)
the Summer Olympics.

7. Yao Ming is one of _____ basketball players
(tall)
in the world.

8. _____ name for soccer in the world is "football."
(common)

9. Running a marathon was one of _____ things
(hard)
I've ever done.

10. In your opinion, what is _____ sport?
(interesting)

Yao Ming

EXERCISE 4 **ABOUT YOU** **Write a superlative sentence giving your opinion about each of the following items. You may find a partner and compare your answers to your partner's answers.**

EXAMPLES big problem in the world today
I think the biggest problem in the world today is hunger.

big problem in the U.S. today
I think crime is one of the biggest problems in the U.S. today.

1. good way to make friends

_____

2. quick way to learn a language

_____

3. good thing about life in the U.S.

_____

4. bad thing about life in the U.S.

_____

5. big problem in (*choose a country*)

_____

EXERCISE 5 **ABOUT YOU** Write superlative sentences about your experience with the words given. Use the present perfect form + *ever* after the superlative.

EXAMPLE big / city / visit

London is the biggest city I have ever visited.
_____

1. tall / building / visit

_____

2. beautiful / actress / see

_____

3. difficult / subject / study

_____

4. far / distance / travel

_____

5. bad / food / eat

_____

6. good / vacation / have

_____

7. good / athlete / see

_____

8. hard / job / have

_____

9. interesting / sporting event / see

_____

EXERCISE 6 **ABOUT YOU** Fill in the blanks.

EXAMPLE   _Swimming across a lake alone at night_____

was one of the most dangerous things I've ever done.

1. _____

is one of the most foolish things I've ever done.

2. _____

is one of the hardest decisions I've ever made.

3. _____

is one of the most dangerous things I've ever done.

12.4 Superlatives and Word Order

EXAMPLES	EXPLANATION
Superlative Noun **Adjective Phrase** Who is **the best American golfer**? **Superlative** **Adjective Noun** What is **the most popular sport** in the world? **Superlative Noun** In golf, the winner scores **the fewest points**.	A superlative adjective comes **before** a noun or noun phrase.
Football is **the most popular sport** in the U.S. OR **The most popular sport** in the U.S. is football.	When the verb *be* connects a noun to a superlative adjective + noun, there are two possible word orders.
Superlative **Verb Adverb** Interest in soccer **is growing the most quickly** in the U.S. **Verb Superlative** **Phrase Adverb** I **watch soccer the most frequently**.	We put superlative adverbs **after** the verb or verb phrase.
Verb Superlative Tiger Woods **plays the best**. **Verb Phrase Superlative** Fans **love Tiger Woods the most**.	We put *the most, the least, the best,* and *the worst* **after** a verb (phrase).

EXERCISE 7 **ABOUT YOU** Name the person who is the superlative in your family in each of the following categories.

EXAMPLE works hard
My mother works the hardest in my family.

1. drives well
2. lives far from me
3. speaks English confidently
4. spends a lot of money
5. is well dressed
6. watches a lot of TV

7. worries a lot
8. lives well
9. works hard
10. is athletic
11. is a big sports fan
12. is learning English quickly

Americans' Attitude Toward Soccer

Before You Read

1. Are you interested in soccer? If so, what is your favorite team?
2. Should children learn to play a sport in school? Why or why not?

CD 4, TR 08

Read the following magazine article. Pay special attention to comparisons.

Soccer is by far the most popular sport in the world. Almost every country has a professional league. In many countries, top international soccer players are **as well-known as** rock stars or actors. However, in 1994, when the World Cup soccer competition was held in the U.S., there was not a lot of interest in soccer among Americans. Many people said that soccer was boring.

Recently, Americans' attitude toward soccer has been changing. In 1999, when the Women's World Cup was played in the U.S., there was **more** interest than ever before. Little by little, soccer is becoming **more popular** in the U.S. The number of children playing soccer is growing. In fact, soccer is growing **faster** than any other sport. For elementary school children, soccer is now the number two sport after basketball. **More** kids play soccer than baseball. Many coaches believe that soccer is **easier** to play than baseball or basketball, and that there aren't **as many** injuries **as** with sports such as hockey or football.

Interest in professional soccer in the U.S. is still much **lower** than in other countries. The number of Americans who watch professional basketball, football, or hockey is still much **higher** than the number who watch Major League Soccer. However, **the more** parents show interest in their children's soccer teams, **the more** they will become interested in professional soccer.

12.5 Comparatives

We use the comparative form to compare two items.

EXAMPLES	EXPLANATION

Soccer players are **shorter than** basketball players.
Interest in soccer is growing **faster than** interest in any other sport.
	Form:
	  short adjective + -er + than
	  short adverb + -er + than

Basketball is **more popular than** soccer in the U.S.
Interest in soccer is growing **more quickly than** interest in hockey.
	Form:
	  more + longer adjective + than
	  more + -ly adverb + than

My brother plays soccer **better than** I do. He can kick the ball **farther than** I can.	Some comparative forms are irregular. See 12.3 for more information about irregular forms.
Basketball is popular in the U.S., but football is **more popular.** Michael Jordan is tall, but Yao Ming is **taller.**	Omit than if the second item of comparison is not included.
Interest in soccer is *much* lower in the U.S. than in other countries. I like soccer *a little* better than I like baseball.	*Much* or *a little* can come before a comparative form.
Formal: You are taller than **I am.** **Informal:** You are taller than **me.** **Formal:** I can play soccer better than **he can.** **Informal:** I can play soccer better than **him.**	When a pronoun follows *than*, the correct form is the subject pronoun (*he, she, I,* etc.). Usually an auxiliary verb follows (*is, do, did, can,* etc.). Informally, many Americans use the object pronoun (*him, her, me,* etc.) after *than*. An auxiliary verb does not follow.
The more they practice, **the better** they play. **The older** you are, **the harder** it is to learn a new sport.	We can use two comparisons in one sentence to show cause and result.

EXERCISE **8** **Circle the correct word to complete each statement.**

EXAMPLE   In the U.S., soccer is (*more* / (*less*)) popular than basketball.

1. Football players have (*more* / *fewer*) injuries than soccer players.

2. In the U.S., soccer is growing (*faster* / *slower*) than any other sport.

3. In 1999, there was (*more* / *less*) interest in soccer than in 1994.

4. Professional soccer is (*more* / *less*) popular in the U.S. than in other countries.

5. In the U.S., soccer players are (*more* / *less*) famous than movie stars.

EXERCISE 9 Fill in the blanks with the comparative form of the word in parentheses ( ). Include *than* when necessary.

EXAMPLE In the U.S., basketball is ___more popular than___ soccer.
(popular)

1. Tall people are often _____ basketball players (good)

   _____ short people.

2. Golf is a _____ sport than soccer. (slow)

3. Which do you think is _____, skiing or surfing? (difficult)

4. A soccer ball is _____ a tennis ball. (large)

5. Children learn sports _____ adults. (easily)

6. People who exercise a lot are in _____ shape (good)

   _____ people who don't.

7. Do you think soccer is _____ football? (interesting)

8. Do you think soccer is _____ baseball? (exciting)

EXERCISE 10 Compare adults to children. Talk in general terms. You may discuss your answers.

EXAMPLE tall
Adults are taller than children.

1. polite
2. friendly
3. formal
4. playful

5. responsible
6. serious
7. curious
8. happy

EXERCISE 11 **ABOUT YOU** Compare the U.S. and your native country (or a place you know well). Explain your response.

EXAMPLES

cars
Cars are cheaper in the U.S. Most people in my native country can't afford a car.

education
Education is better in my native country. Everyone must finish high school.

1. rent
2. housing
3. cars

4. education
5. medical care
6. food

7. gasoline
8. the government
9. clothes (or fashions)

12.6 Comparatives and Word Order

EXAMPLES	EXPLANATION
Comparative Be Adjective Football **is more popular** than soccer in the U.S. Linking Comparative Verb Adjective Football **looks more dangerous** than soccer.	Put the comparative adjective after the verb *be* or other linking verbs: *seem, feel, look, sound,* etc.
Verb Comparative Phrase Adverb Woods **played golf more successfully** than his father. Comparative Verb Adverb Soccer **is growing faster** than any other sport.	Put the comparative adverb **after** the verb (phrase).
Comparative Noun There is **less interest** in hockey than there is in golf. Comparative Noun Soccer players have **fewer injuries** than football players.	We can put *more, less, fewer, better,* and *worse* **before** a noun.
Verb Phrase Comparative My sister **likes soccer more** than I do. Verb Phrase Comparative I **play soccer worse** than my sister does.	You can put *more, less, better, worse,* and other comparative forms **after** a verb (phrase).

EXERCISE **12** **Find the mistakes with word order and correct them. Not every sentence has a mistake. If the sentence is correct, write *C*.**

EXAMPLES   A football team has players *more* than a baseball team.

A golf ball is smaller than a tennis ball. *C*

1. A basketball player is taller than a gymnast.
2. A baseball game has action less than a soccer game.
3. Football players use more padding than soccer players.
4. Tiger Woods more remarkably plays golf than most other players.
5. I more like baseball than basketball.
6. Team A won more games than Team B.
7. Team A better played than Team B.

EXERCISE **13** **ABOUT YOU** **Compare yourself to another person, or compare two people you know using these verb phrases.**

EXAMPLE   drive well
I drive better than my brother.

1. dress stylishly
2. work hard
3. spend a lot
4. speak English well
5. worry a little
6. live comfortably
7. have freedom
8. have an easy life
9. exercise a lot

EXERCISE **14** **ABOUT YOU** **Compare this school to another school you attended. Use *better*, *worse*, *more*, *less*, or *fewer* before the noun.**

EXAMPLE   classroom / space
This classroom has more space than a classroom in my native country.

1. class / students
2. school / courses
3. teachers / experience
4. library / books
5. school / facilities[2]
6. school / teachers

EXERCISE **15** **Fill in the blanks with the comparative or superlative form of the word in parentheses ( ). Include *than* or *the* when necessary.**

EXAMPLES   In the U.S., baseball is ___more popular than___ soccer.
                                                        (popular)

Baseball is one of ___the most popular___ sports in the U.S.
                                        (popular)

1. A tennis ball is _____ a baseball.
                                    (soft)

[2]*Facilities* are things we use, such as a swimming pool, cafeteria, library, exercise room, or student union.

2. An athlete who wins the gold medal is _____ athlete
(good)

in his or her sport.

3. Who is _____ basketball player in the world?
(tall)

4. I am _____ in baseball _____ in
(interested)

basketball.

5. In my opinion, soccer is _____ sport.
(exciting)

6. Weightlifters are _____ than golfers.
(muscular)

7. Golf is a _____ sport _____ soccer.
(slow)

8. A basketball team has _____ players
(few)

_____ a baseball team.

9. Even though January is _____ month of the year,
(cold)

football players play during this month.

10. My friend and I both jog. I run _____ than my friend.
(far)

11. Who's a _____ soccer player—you or your brother?
(good)

An Amazing Athlete

CD 4, TR 09

Before
You Read

1. Can people with disabilities do well in sports?

2. Why do people want to climb the tallest mountain in the world?

Read the following magazine article. Pay special attention to comparisons.

Erik Weihenmayer is **as tough as** any mountain climber. In 2001 he made his way to the top of the highest mountain in the world—Mount Everest—at the age of 33. But Erik is **different from** other mountain climbers in one important way—he is completely blind. He is the first sightless person to reach the top of the tallest mountain.

Erik was an athletic child who lost his vision in his early teens. At first he refused to use a cane or learn Braille, insisting he could do **as well as** any teenager. But he finally came to accept his disability. He couldn't play **the same** sports **as** he used to. He would never be able to play basketball or catch a football again. But then he discovered wrestling, a sport where sight was not **as important as** feel and touch. Then, at 16, he discovered rock climbing, which **was like** wrestling in some ways; a wrestler and a rock climber get information through touch. Rock climbing led to mountain climbing, the greatest challenge of his life.

Teammates climbing with Erik say that he isn't **different from** a sighted mountaineer. He has **as much training as** the others. He is **as strong as** the rest. The major difference is he is not **as thin as** most climbers. But his strong upper body, flexibility, mental toughness, and ability to tolerate physical pain make him a perfect climber. The only accommodation for Erik's blindness is to place bells on the jackets of his teammates so that he can follow them easily.

Climbing Mount Everest was a challenge for every climber on Erik's team. The reaction to the mountain air for Erik was **the same as** it was for his teammates: lack of oxygen causes the heart to beat slower than usual, and the brain does not function **as clearly as** normal. In some ways, Erik had an advantage over his teammates: as they got near the top, the vision of all climbers was restricted. So at a certain altitude, all his teammates **were like** Erik—nearly blind.

To climb Mount Everest is an achievement for any athlete. Erik Weihenmayer showed that his disability wasn't **as important as** his ability.

12.7 As . . . As

EXAMPLES	EXPLANATION
Erik is **as strong as** his teammates. At high altitudes, the brain doesn't function **as clearly as** normal. Erik can climb mountains **as well as** sighted climbers.	We can show that two things are equal or unequal in some way by using: *(not)* as + adjective/adverb + *as*.
Erik is not **as thin as** most climbers. Skiing is not **as difficult as** mountain climbing.	When we make a comparison of unequal items, we put the lesser item first.
Baseball is popular in the U.S. Soccer is not **as popular**.	Omit the second *as* if the second item of comparison is omitted.

(continued)

Usage Note: A very common expression is *as soon as possible*. Some people say *A.S.A.P.* for short.

> I'd like to see you *as soon as possible*.
> I'd like to see you *A.S.A.P.*

EXERCISE 16 **Tell if the statement is true or false. Write *T* for true and *F* for false.**

EXAMPLE   In wrestling, the sense of sight is as important as the sense of touch. **F**

1. Rock climbing is not as dangerous as mountain climbing.
2. At high altitudes, you can't think as clearly as you can at lower altitudes.
3. Erik was not as strong as his teammates.
4. When Erik became blind, he wanted to do as well as any other teenager.
5. Erik could not go as far as his teammates on Mount Everest.
6. Erik was as prepared for the climb as his teammates.

EXERCISE 17   **ABOUT YOU** **Compare yourself to another person. (Or compare two people you know.) Use the following adjectives and *as . . . as*. You may add a comparative statement if there is inequality.**

EXAMPLES   thin
I'm not as thin as my sister. (She's thinner than I am.)

smart
My mother is as smart as my father.

1. old	4. patient	7. religious	10. talkative
2. educated	5. lazy	8. friendly	11. athletic
3. intelligent	6. tall	9. strong	12. interested in sports

EXERCISE 18   **ABOUT YOU** **Use the following phrases to compare yourself to the teacher.**

EXAMPLE   speak Spanish well
The teacher doesn't speak Spanish as well as I do. (I speak Spanish better.)

1. arrive at class promptly
2. work hard in class
3. understand American customs well
4. speak quietly
5. speak English fluently

6. understand a foreigner's problems well

7. write neatly

8. speak fast

12.8 As Many/Much . . . As

EXAMPLES	EXPLANATION
Soccer players don't have **as many injuries as** football players. Erik had **as much training as** his teammates.	We can show that two things are equal or not equal in quantity by using: *(not) as many* + count noun + *as* OR *(not) as much* + noncount noun + *as*.
I don't play soccer **as much as** I used to. She doesn't like sports **as much as** her husband does.	We can use *as much as* after a verb phrase.

EXERCISE 19 **ABOUT YOU** *PART A:* **Fill in the blanks.**

EXAMPLE I drive about ____30____ miles a week.

(number)

1. I'm _____ tall.

(feet/inches OR centimeters)

2. The highest level of education that I have completed is

_____.

(high school, bachelor's degree, master's degree, doctorate)

3. I work _____ hours a week.

(number)

4. I study _____ hours a day.

(number)

5. I exercise _____ days a week.

(number)

6. I'm taking _____ courses now.

(number)

7. I have _____ siblings.[3]

(number)

8. I live _____ miles from this school.

(number)

[3]*Siblings* are a person's brothers and sisters.

PART B: **Find a partner and compare your answers to your partner's answers. Write statements with the words given and *(not) as . . . as* or *(not) as much / many as.***

EXAMPLE   drive ___I don't drive as much as Lisa.___

1. tall _____

2. have education _____

3. work _____

4. study _____

5. exercise frequently _____

6. take courses _____

7. have siblings _____

8. live far from school _____

EXERCISE **20**   **Compare yourself to another person, or compare two people you know. Use *as many as* or *as much as.***

EXAMPLE   show emotion
My mom doesn't show as much emotion as my grandmother. (My grandmother shows more emotion than my mom.)

1. earn	5. like to go shopping
2. spend money	6. have responsibilities
3. talk	7. have freedom
4. gossip	8. have free time

EXERCISE **21**   **Compare this school and another school you attended. Use *as many as.***

EXAMPLE   classrooms
This school doesn't have as many classrooms as King College. (King College has more classrooms.)

1. teachers	3. floors (or stories)	5. exams
2. classrooms	4. English courses	6. students

EXERCISE **22**   **Make a comparison between this city and another city you know well using the categories below.**

EXAMPLE   public transportation ___The buses are cleaner in Boston than in this city.___

OR   ___The buses in this city are not as crowded as the buses in Boston.___

1. traffic _____

2. people _____

3. gardens and parks _____

4. public transportation _____

5. museums _____

6. universities _____

7. houses _____

8. buildings _____

9. stores or shopping _____

12.9 The Same . . . As

EXAMPLES	EXPLANATION
Pattern A: Erik had **the same ability as** his teammates. A soccer ball isn't **the same shape as** a football.	We can show that two things are equal or not equal in some way by using: *(not) the same* + noun + *as*.
Pattern B: Erik and his teammates had **the same ability**. A soccer ball and a football aren't **the same shape**.	Omit *as* in Pattern B.

Language Note: We can make statements of equality or inequality with many nouns, such as *size, shape, color, value, religion,* or *nationality*.

EXERCISE 23   **Make statements with *the same . . . as* using the words given.**

EXAMPLE   a golf ball / a tennis ball (size)

A golf ball isn't the same size as a tennis ball. _____

1. a soccer ball / a volleyball (shape)

   _____

2. a soccer player / a basketball player (height)

   _____

3. an amateur athlete / a professional athlete (ability)

   _____

4. a soccer player / a football player (weight)

   _____

5. team A's uniforms / team B's uniforms (color)

   _____

EXERCISE **24** Talk about two relatives or friends of yours. Compare them using the words given.

EXAMPLE age
My mother and my father aren't the same age.
OR
My mother isn't the same age as my father. (My father is older than my mother.)

1. age
2. height
3. weight
4. nationality
5. religion
6. (have) level of education

EXERCISE **25** **ABOUT YOU** Work with a partner. Make a true affirmative or negative statement about you and your partner with the words given.

EXAMPLES the same nationality
I'm not the same nationality as Alex. I'm Colombian, and he's Russian.

the same color shoes
Martina's shoes are the same color as my shoes. They're brown.

1. the same hair color
2. the same eye color
3. (speak) the same language
4. (like) the same sports
5. (have) the same level of English
6. the same nationality

12.10 Equality with Nouns or Adjectives

For equality or inequality with nouns, use *(not) the same . . . as*. For equality or inequality with adjectives and adverbs, use *(not) as . . . as* or the comparative form.

NOUN	ADJECTIVE	EXAMPLES
height	tall, short	A soccer player is not **the same height as** a basketball player. A soccer player is not **as tall as** a basketball player. A soccer player is **shorter**.
age	old, young	He's not **the same age as** his wife. He's not **as old as** his wife. His wife is **older**.

NOUN	ADJECTIVE	EXAMPLES
weight	heavy, light	The wrestler in blue is not **the same weight as** the wrestler in red. The wrestler in blue is not **as heavy as** the wrestler in red. The wrestler in blue is **lighter.**
length	long, short	This shelf is not **the same length as** that shelf. This shelf is not **as long as** that shelf. This shelf is **shorter.**
price	expensive, cheap	This car is not **the same price as** that car. This car is not **as expensive as** that car. This car is **cheaper.**
size	big, small	Those shoes are not **the same size as** these shoes. Those shoes are not **as big as** these shoes. Those shoes are **smaller.**

EXERCISE **26** **Change the following sentences to use *as . . . as* and then the comparative form. Answers may vary.**

EXAMPLE   Lesson 11 isn't the same length as Lesson 12.

Lesson 11 is _____ **not as long as Lesson 12. Lesson 11 is shorter.** _____

1. I'm not the same height as my brother.

   My brother is _____

2. You're not the same age as your husband.

   You're _____

3. I'm not the same height as a basketball player.

   A basketball player is _____

4. My left foot isn't the same size as my right foot.

   My right foot is _____

5. My brother isn't the same weight as I am.

   My brother is _____

Football and Soccer

1. Which do you like better, football or soccer?

2. How are soccer players different from football players?

 CD 4, TR 10

Read the following Web article. Pay special attention to similarities and differences.

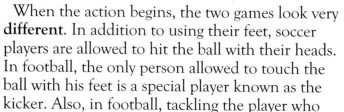

http://www.all*sports.com

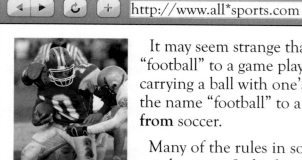

It may seem strange that Americans give the name "football" to a game played mostly by throwing and carrying a ball with one's hands. But Americans give the name "football" to a sport that is very **different from** soccer.

Many of the rules in soccer and American football are the **same**. In both games, there are 11 players on each side, and a team scores its points by getting the ball past the goal of the other team. The playing fields for both teams are also very much **alike**.

When the action begins, the two games look very **different**. In addition to using their feet, soccer players are allowed to hit the ball with their heads. In football, the only person allowed to touch the ball with his feet is a special player known as the kicker. Also, in football, tackling the player who has the ball is not only allowed but encouraged, whereas tackling any player in soccer will get the tackler thrown out of the game.

Football players and soccer players don't **dress alike** or even **look alike** in many ways. Since blocking and tackling are a big part of American football, the players are often very large and muscular and wear heavy padding and helmets. Soccer players, on the other hand, are usually thinner and wear shorts and polo shirts. This gives them more freedom of movement to show off the fancy footwork that makes soccer such a popular game around the world.

While both games are very **different**, both have a large number of fans that enjoy the exciting action.

12.11 Similarity with *Like* and *Alike*

We can show that two things are similar (or not) with *like* and *alike*.

EXAMPLES	EXPLANATION
Pattern A: A soccer player **looks like** a rugby player. A soccer player doesn't **dress like** a football player.	**Pattern A:** Noun 1 + verb + *like* + Noun 2
Pattern B: A soccer player and a rugby player **look alike.** A soccer player and a football player don't **dress alike.**	**Pattern B:** Noun 1 and Noun 2 + verb + *alike*
Language Note: We often use the sense perception verbs (*look, sound, smell, taste, feel,* and *seem*) with *like* and *alike*. We can also use other verbs with *like: act like, sing like, dress like,* etc.	

Rugby

Soccer

Football

EXERCISE 27 **Make a statement with the words given. Use *like* or *alike*.**

EXAMPLE taste / decaf [4] / regular coffee
Decaf tastes like regular coffee (to me).
OR
Decaf and regular coffee taste alike (to me).

1. taste / diet cola / regular cola
2. taste / 2% milk / whole milk
3. look / an American classroom / a classroom in another country

---

[4]*Decaf* coffee doesn't contain caffeine.

4. sound / Asian music / American music

5. feel / polyester / silk

6. smell / cologne / perfume

7. look / salt / sugar

8. taste / salt / sugar

9. act / American teachers / teachers in other countries

10. dress / American teenagers / teenagers in other countries

EXERCISE **28** **Fill in the blanks. Practice using *like* and *alike*. In some cases, more than one answer is possible.**

EXAMPLE Players on the same team dress _____ *alike* _____.

1. Identical twins _____ alike.

2. Americans and people from England don't sound _____. They have different accents.

3. My daughter is only 15 years old, but she _____ an adult. She's very responsible and hardworking.

4. My son is only 16 years old, but he _____ an adult. He's tall and has a beard.

5. Teenagers often wear the same clothing as their friends. They like to _____.

6. Soccer players don't look _____ football players at all.

7. Do you think I'll ever _____ an American, or will I always have an accent?

8. In some schools, children wear a uniform. They _____ alike.

9. My children learned English very quickly. Now they sound _____ Americans. They have no accent at all.

10. Dogs don't _____ cats at all. Dogs are very friendly. Cats are more distant.

12.12 Be Like

We can show that two things are similar (or not) in internal characteristics with *be like* and *be alike*.

EXAMPLES	EXPLANATION
Pattern A: For Erik, mountain climbing **is like** wrestling in some ways. Touch is more important than sight. Erik **was like** his teammates in many ways—strong, well trained, mentally tough, and able to tolerate pain.	**Pattern A:** Noun 1 + *be like* + Noun 2
Pattern B: For Erik, wrestling and mountain climbing **are alike** in some ways. Erik and his teammates **were alike** in many ways.	**Pattern B:** Noun 1 and Noun 2 + *be alike*
Compare: a. Erik **looks like** an athlete. He's tall and strong. b. Erik **is like** his teammates. He has a lot of experience and training.	a. Use *look like* to describe an outward appearance. b. Use *be like* to describe an internal characteristic.

EXERCISE 29 **ABOUT YOU** Work with a student from another country. Ask a question with the words given. Use *be like*. The other student will answer.

EXAMPLE families in the U.S. / families in your native country

> **A:** Are families in the U.S. like families in your native country?
> **B:** No, they aren't. Families in my native country are very big. Family members live close to each other.

1. an English class in the U.S. / an English class in your native country
2. your house (or apartment) in the U.S. / your house (or apartment) in your native country
3. the weather in this city / the weather in your hometown
4. food in your country / American food
5. women's clothes in your native country / women's clothes in the U.S.
6. a college in your native country / a college in the U.S.
7. American teachers / teachers in your native country
8. American athletes / athletes in your native country

12.13 Same or Different

We show that two things are the same (or not) by using *the same as*. We show that two things are different by using *different from*.

EXAMPLES	EXPLANATION
Pattern A: Football is **not the same as** soccer. Football is **different from** soccer.	**Pattern A:** Noun 1 is *(not) the same as* Noun 2. Noun 1 is *different from* Noun 2.
Pattern B: Football and soccer are **not the same**. Football and soccer are **different**.	**Pattern B:** Noun 1 and Noun 2 are *(not) the same*. Noun 1 and Noun 2 are *different*.
Language Note: You will hear some Americans say *different <u>than</u>*.	

EXERCISE 30 **Tell if the two items are the same or different.**

EXAMPLES boxing, wrestling
Boxing and wrestling are different.

fall, autumn
Fall is the same as autumn.

1. Michael Jordan, Michael Phelps
2. a century, one hundred years
3. rock climbing, mountain climbing
4. a kilometer, 1,000 meters
5. L.A., Los Angeles
6. a mile, a kilometer
7. football, rugby
8. football rules, soccer rules

EXERCISE 31 **Fill in the blanks in the following conversation.**

CD 4, TR 11

A: I heard that you have a twin brother.

B: Yes, I do.

A: Do you and your brother look _____*alike*_____?

(example)

B: No. He _____ (1) _____ look _____ (2) _____ me at all.

A: But you're twins.

B: We're fraternal twins. That's different _____ (3) _____ identical

twins, who have the _____ (4) _____ genetic code. We're just

brothers who were born at _____ (5) _____ time. We're not

even the same _____ (6) _____. I'm much taller than he is.

404 Lesson 12

A: But you're _____ in many ways, aren't you?
(7)

B: No. We're completely _____. I'm athletic and I'm on
(8)

the high school football team, but David hates sports. He's a much

_____ student than I am. He's much more
(9)

_____ our mother, who loves to read and learn
(10)

new things, and I _____ our father, who's athletic
(11)

and loves to build things.

A: What about your character?

B: I'm outgoing and he's very shy. Also we don't dress _____
(12)

at all. He likes to wear neat, conservative clothes, but I prefer torn jeans

and T-shirts.

A: From your description, it _____ like you're not even
(13)

from the same family.

B: We have one thing in common. We were both interested in

_____ girl at school. We both asked her out, but she
(14)

didn't want to go out with either one of us!

EXERCISE 32 **This is a conversation between two women. Fill in the blanks with an appropriate word to complete the comparisons.**

CD 4, TR 12

A: In the winter months, my husband doesn't pay as _____**much**_____
(example)

attention to me _____ he does to his football games.
(1)

B: Many women have the same problem _____ you do.
(2)

These women are called "football widows" because they lose their

husbands during football season.

A: I feel _____ a widow.
(3)

My husband is in front of the TV all day

on the weekends. In addition to the

football games, there are pre-game shows.

These shows last _____ long as the game itself.
(4)

(continued)

B: I know what you mean. He's no different _____ my (5)

husband. During football season, my husband is _____ (6)

interested in watching TV _____ he is in me. He looks (7)

_____ a robot sitting in front of the TV. When I (8)

complain, he tells me to sit down and join him.

A: It sounds _____ all men act _____ (9) (10)

during football season.

B: To tell the truth, I don't like football at all.

A: I don't either. I think soccer is much _____ interesting (11)

than football.

B: Soccer is very different _____ football. I think the (12)

action is _____ exciting. And it's more fun to watch (13)

the footwork of the soccer players. Football players look

_____ big monsters with their helmets and padded (14)

shoulders. They don't look handsome at all.

A: Soccer is not _____ popular in the U.S. (15)

_____ it is in other countries. I wonder why. (16)

B: What's your favorite team?

A: I like the Chicago Fire.

B: In my opinion they're not _____ good as the Los (17)

Angeles Galaxy. But to tell the truth, I'm not very interested in sports

at all. When our husbands start watching football next season, let's do

our favorite sport: shopping. We can spend _____ (18)

time shopping as they spend in front of the TV.

A: I was just thinking the same thing! You and I think

_____. We're football widows, but our husbands can be (19)

"shopping widowers."

Summary of Lesson 12

1. **Simple, Comparative, and Superlative Forms**

   SHORT WORDS

   Jacob is **tall**.
   Mark is **taller than** Jacob.
   Bart is **the tallest** member of the basketball team.

   LONG WORDS

   Golf is **popular** in the U.S.
   Baseball is **more popular than** golf.
   Soccer is **the most popular** game in the world.

2. **Other Kinds of Comparisons**

   She looks **as young as** her daughter.
   She speaks English **as fluently as** her husband.
   She is **the same age as** her husband.
   She and her husband are **the same age**.
   She works **as many hours as** her husband.
   She doesn't have **as much time as** her husband.
   She works **as much as** her husband.

3. **Comparisons with** *Like*

   She's **like** her mother. (She and her mother **are alike**.) They're both athletic.
   She **looks like** her sister. (She and her sister **look alike**.) They're identical twins.
   Lemons **don't taste like** limes. (They don't taste **alike**.)
   Western music doesn't **sound like** Asian music. (They don't **sound alike**.)

4. **Comparisons with** *Same* **and** *Different*

   Football is **different from** soccer.
   My uniform is **the same as** my teammates' uniforms.

Editing Advice

1. Don't use *more* and *-er* together.

   He is ~~more~~ older than his teacher.

2. Use *than* before the second item of comparison.

        than
   He is younger ~~that~~ his wife.

3. Use *the* before a superlative form.

the
The Nile is ˄ longest river in the world.

4. Use a plural noun in the phrase "one of the [superlative] [nouns]."

cities
Chicago is one of the biggest ~~city~~ in the U.S.

5. Use the correct word order.

talks more
She ~~more talks~~ than her husband.

more time
I have ~~time more~~ than you.

6. Use *be like* for inward similarity. Use *look like* for an outward similarity.

s
He ~~is~~ look ˄ like his brother. They both have blue eyes and dark hair.

He is ~~look~~ like his sister. They are both talented musicians.

7. Use the correct negative for *be like, look like, sound like, feel like,* etc.

don't
I'm ~~not~~ look like my father.

does
He ~~is~~ not act like a professional athlete.

Editing Quiz

Some of the shaded words and phrases have mistakes. Find the mistakes and correct them. If the shaded words are correct, write C.

s
Soccer is one of my favorite sport. In fact, it is probably
C   *(example)*   ˄
the most popular sport in the world. I know Americans prefer football,
(example)
but for me soccer is much more interesting that football. In fact, I think
    (1)   *(2)*
soccer is the more exciting sport in the world. There are some good
    (3)
American teams, but they aren't as good as some of the European
          (4)
teams. I think Italy has one of the best team. In South America, Brazil
        (5)   *(6)*
has a very good team.
    (7)

The name "football" is confusing. "Football" is sounds like you use only
                                                            (8)
your feet, but football players carry the ball. A football and a soccer ball don't

look alike at all. A soccer ball is round, but a football isn't. The game of
(9)
football isn't look like the game of soccer at all. These sports are
            (10)
completely different. The players are different too. Soccer players are not

the same big as football players. There is just one similarity: a soccer team
(11)
has the same number of players than a football team.
    (12)   (13)

    I love to watch soccer, but I like to play it even more. When I lived in

my country I played more better because I more practiced. I played every
                     (14)   (15)
weekend. But here I don't have as much time than before. I watch it on
                               (16)   (17)
TV but it isn't as much fun as playing it.
            (18)

Lesson 12 Test/Review

PART **1** **Fill in the blanks with the comparative or superlative form of the
word in parentheses ( ). Include *than* or *the* when necessary.**

1. Soccer is _____ sport in the world.
                    (popular)

2. In the U.S., football is _____ soccer.
                                    (popular)

3. Erik Weihenmayer is one of _____ athletes in the world.
                                      (interesting)

4. Weihenmayer is _____ other mountain climbers.
                          (heavy)

5. He found climbing _____ wrestling.
                            (exciting)

6. Climbing Mount Everest is _____ climbing any
                                    (difficult)
   other mountain.

7. Mount Everest is _____ mountain in the world.
                          (tall)

8. Tiger Woods played golf _____ his father.
                                  (good)

9. In golf, the player who has _____ scores wins.
                                      (low)

10. In the 2008 Olympics, Michael Phelps swam _____.
                                                      (fast)

PART 2 **Fill in the blanks.**

EXAMPLE A tangerine is _____the same_____ color _____as_____ an orange.

1. She's 35 years old. Her husband is 35 years old. She and her husband are _____ age.

2. She earns $30,000 a year. Her husband earns $35,000. She doesn't earn as _____ her husband.

3. The little girl _____ like her mother. They both have brown eyes and curly black hair.

4. My name is Sophia Weiss. My teacher's name is Judy Weiss. We have _____ last name.

5. Chinese food is different _____ American food.

6. A dime isn't the same _____ a nickel. A dime is smaller.

7. She is as tall as her husband. They are the same _____.

8. A grapefruit doesn't _____ like an orange. An orange is sweeter.

9. She _____ like her husband in many ways. They're both intelligent and hardworking. They both like sports.

10. **A:** Are you like your mother?
    B: Oh, no. We're not _____ at all! We're completely different.

11. Please finish this test _____ possible.

12. *Borrow* and *lend* don't have _____ meaning. *Borrow* means take. *Lend* means give.

13. My two sisters look _____. In fact, some people think they're twins.

Expansion

Classroom Activities

❶ **Work with a partner. Find some differences between the two of you. Then write five sentences that compare you and your partner. Share your answers in a small group or with the whole class.**

EXAMPLES   I'm taller than Alex.
Alex is taking more classes than I am.

❷ **Form a small group (about 3–5 people) with students from different native countries, if possible. Make comparisons about your native countries. Include a superlative statement. (If all the students in your class are from the same native country, compare cities in your native country.)**

EXAMPLES   Cuba is closer to the U.S. than Peru is.
China has the largest population.
Cuba doesn't have as many resources as China.

❸ **Work with a partner. Choose one of the categories below, and compare two examples from this category. Use any type of comparative method. Write four sentences. Share your answers with the class.**

a. countries	**f.** animals
b. cars	**g.** types of transportation
c. restaurants	**h.** schools
d. teachers	**i.** sports
e. cities	**j.** athletes

EXAMPLE   animals

A dog is different from a cat in many ways.

A dog can't jump as high as a cat.

A dog is a better pet than a cat, in my opinion.

A cat is not as friendly as a dog.

4 Compare the U.S. to another country you know. Tell if the statement is true in the U.S. or in the other country. Form a small group and explain your answers to the others in the group.

	Country _____	The U.S.
People have more free time.		
People have more political freedom.		
Families are smaller.		
Children are more polite.		
Teenagers have more freedom.		
People are friendlier.		
The government is more stable.		
Health care is better.		
There is more crime.		
There are more poor people.		
People are generally happier.		
People are more open about their problems.		
Friendship is more important.		
Women have more freedom.		
Schools are better.		
Job opportunities are better.		
Athletes make more money.		
Children have more fun.		
People dress more stylishly.		
Families are closer.		
People are healthier.		

⑤ Look at the list of jobs below. Use the superlative form to name a job that matches each description. You may discuss your answers in a small group or with the entire class.

EXAMPLE   interesting
In my opinion, a psychologist has the most interesting job.

coach   referee
psychologist   letter carrier
computer programmer   athlete
high school teacher   actress
factory worker   photojournalist
doctor   firefighter
police officer   politician
engineer   nurse

(*you may add other professions*)

a. interesting _____

b. dangerous _____

c. easy _____

d. tiring _____

e. dirty _____

f. boring _____

g. exciting _____

h. important _____

i. challenging _____

j. difficult _____

Talk
About It

❶ Do athletes in other countries make a lot of money?

❷ Do children in most countries participate in sports? Which sports?

❸ Why do you think soccer isn't as popular in the U.S. as it is in other countries?

❹ Do you watch the Olympic Games? What's your favorite sport to watch?

Write

About It **Write a short composition comparing one of the sets of items below:**

- two stores where you shop for groceries
- watching a movie at home and at a movie theater
- you and your parents
- football and soccer (or any two sports)
- life in the U.S. (in general) and life in your native country
- schools (including teachers, students, classes, etc.) in the U.S. and schools in your native country
- American families and families in your native country
- clothing styles in the U.S. and your native country

Clothing Styles

People dress differently in my country, Lithuania. Styles are much more formal than in the U.S. People usually wear dressy clothes and shoes to work. Here people wear very informal clothes. It's more important for Americans to be comfortable than to be fashionable . . .

 For more practice using grammar in context, please visit our Web site.

Grammar
Passive Voice and Active Voice

Context
The Law

	EXAMPLES			EXPLANATION
Active	**Subject**	**Active Verb**	**Object**	The **active voice** focuses on the person who performs the action. The subject is active.
	The thief	**stole**	the bicycle.	
	The police	**arrested**	the thief.	
Passive	**Subject**	**Passive Verb**	*By* **Phrase**	The **passive voice** focuses on the receiver or the result of the action. The subject is passive. The person who does the action is in the *by* phrase.
	The bicycle	**was stolen**	*by* the thief.	
	The thief	**was arrested**	*by* the police.	
Passive	**Subject**	**Passive Verb**	**Complement**	Many passive sentences do not contain a *by* phrase.
	The thief	**was taken**	to jail.	
	The bicycle	**will be returned**	tomorrow.	

Jury Duty

Before You Read

1. Have you ever been to court?

2. Have you ever seen a courtroom in a movie or TV show?

CD 4, TR 13

Read the following magazine article. Pay special attention to the passive voice.

All Americans are protected by the Constitution. No one person can decide if a person is guilty of a crime. Every citizen has the right to a trial by jury. When a person **is charged** with a crime, he **is considered** innocent until the jury decides he is guilty.

Most American citizens **are chosen** for jury duty at some time in their lives. How **are** jurors **chosen**? The court gets the names of citizens from lists of taxpayers, licensed drivers, and voters. Many people **are called** to the courthouse for the selection of a jury. From this large number, 12 people **are chosen**. The lawyers and the judge ask each person questions to see if the person is going to be fair. If the person has made any judgment about the case before hearing the facts presented in the trial, he **is** not **selected**. If the juror doesn't understand enough English, he **is** not **selected**. The court needs jurors who can understand the facts and be open-minded. When the final jury selection **is made**, the jurors must raise their right hands and promise to be fair in deciding the case.

Sometimes a trial goes on for several days or more. Jurors **are** not **permitted** to talk with family members and friends about the case. In some cases, jurors **are** not **permitted** to go home until the case is over. They stay in a hotel and **are** not **permitted** to watch TV or read newspapers that give information about the case.

After the jurors hear the case, they have to make a decision. They go to a separate room and talk about what they heard and saw in the courtroom. When they are finished discussing the case, they take a vote.

Jurors **are paid** for their work. They receive a small amount of money per day. Employers must give a worker permission to be on a jury. Being on a jury **is considered** a very serious job.

13.2 The Passive Voice

EXAMPLES			EXPLANATION
	Be	**Past Participle**	The passive voice uses a form of *be* (any tense) + the past participle.
The jurors	**are**	**chosen** from lists.	
My sister	**was**	**selected** to be on a jury.	
The jurors	**will be**	**paid** for jury duty.	
Compare Active (A) and Passive (P): (A) Ms. Smith **paid** her employees at the end of the week. (P) Ms. Smith **was paid** for being a juror.			The verb in active voice (A) shows that the subject (Ms. Smith) performed the action of the verb. The verb in passive voice (P) shows that the subject (Ms. Smith) did not perform the action of the verb.
I was helped **by the lawyer.** My sister was helped **by him** too.			When a performer is included after a passive verb, use *by* + noun or object pronoun.

EXERCISE 1 Read the following sentences. Decide if the underlined verb is active (*A*) or passive (*P*).

EXAMPLES I <u>received</u> a letter from the court.   **A**

I <u>was told</u> to go to court on May 10.   **P**

1. The jury <u>voted</u> at the end of the trial.
2. The jurors <u>received</u> $20 a day.
3. Some jurors <u>were told</u> to go home.
4. Not every juror <u>will be needed</u>.
5. Twelve people <u>were selected</u> for the jury.
6. The judge <u>told</u> the jurors about their responsibilities.
7. My sister <u>has been selected</u> for jury duty three times.
8. You <u>will be paid</u> for jury duty.
9. A juror <u>must be</u> at least 18 years old and an American citizen.
10. The judge and the lawyers <u>ask</u> a lot of questions.

13.3 The Passive Voice—Form and Uses

Form: The passive voice can be used with different tenses and with modals. The tense of the sentence is shown by the verb *be*. Use the past participle with every tense.

TENSE	ACTIVE	PASSIVE (*BE* + PAST PARTICIPLE)
Simple Present	They **take** a vote.	A vote **is taken**.
Simple Past	They **took** a vote.	A vote **was taken**.
Future	They **will take** a vote. They **are going to take** a vote.	A vote **will be taken**. A vote **is going to be taken**.
Present Perfect	They **have taken** a vote.	A vote **has been taken**.
Modal	They **must take** a vote.	A vote **must be taken**.

Language Notes:
1. An adverb can be placed between the auxiliary verb and the main verb.
   The jurors **are** *always* **paid**.
   Noncitizens **are** *never* **selected** for jury duty.
2. If two verbs in the passive voice are connected with *and*, do not repeat *be*.
   The jurors **are taken** to a room and **shown** a film about the court system.

Uses: The passive voice is used more frequently without a performer than with a performer.

EXAMPLES	EXPLANATION
English **is spoken** in the U.S. Independence Day **is celebrated** in July.	The passive voice is used when the action is done by people in general.
The jurors **are given** a lunch break. The jurors **will be paid** at the end of the day. Jurors **are** not **permitted** to talk with family members about the case.	The passive voice is used when the actual person who performs the action is of little or no importance.
a. The criminal **was arrested**. b. The students **will be given** a test on the passive voice.	The passive voice is used when it is obvious who performed the action. In (a), it is obvious that the police arrested the criminal. In (b), it is obvious that the teacher will give a test.
Active: The lawyers **presented** the case yesterday. **Passive:** The case **was presented** in two hours. **Active:** The judge and the lawyers **choose** jurors. **Passive:** People who don't understand English **are** not **chosen**.	The passive voice is used to shift the emphasis from the performer to the receiver of the action.

EXERCISE **2** Change to the passive voice. (Do not include a *by* phrase.)

ACTIVE   PASSIVE

EXAMPLE They chose him.   _____He was chosen._____

1. They will choose him.   _____
2. They always choose you.   _____
3. They can't choose them.   _____
4. They have never chosen us.   _____
5. They didn't choose me.   _____
6. They shouldn't choose her.   _____

EXERCISE 3   **Fill in the blanks with the passive voice of the verb in parentheses ( ). Use the present tense.**

EXAMPLE   Jurors _____*are chosen*_____ from lists.
(choose)

1. Only people over 18 years old _____ for jury duty.
(select)

2. Questionnaires[1] _____ to American citizens.
(send)

3. The questionnaire _____ out and
(fill)

_____.
(return)

4. Many people _____ to the courthouse.
(call)

5. Not everyone _____.
(choose)

6. The jurors _____ a lot of questions.
(ask)

7. Jurors _____ to discuss the case with outsiders.
(not/permit)

8. Jurors _____ a paycheck at the end of the day for
(give)

their work.

EXERCISE 4   **Fill in the blanks with the passive voice of the verb in parentheses ( ). Use the past tense.**

EXAMPLE   I _____*was sent*_____ a letter.
(send)

1. I _____ to go to the courthouse on Fifth Street.
(tell)

2. My name _____.
(call)

3. I _____ a form to fill out.
(give)

4. A video about jury duty _____ on a large TV.
(show)

5. The jurors _____ to the third floor of the building.
(take)

6. I _____ a lot of questions by the lawyers.
(ask)

7. I _____.
(not/choose)

8. I _____ home before noon.
(send)

[1]A *questionnaire* is a list of questions about a topic.

EXERCISE 5   Fill in the blanks with the passive voice of the verb in parentheses ( ).
Use the present perfect tense.

EXAMPLE   The jurors ___have been given___ a lot of information.
(give)

1. Many articles _____ about the courts.
(write)

2. Many movies _____ about the courts.
(make)

3. Many people _____ for jury duty.
(choose)

4. Your name _____ for jury duty.
(select)

5. The jurors _____ for their work.
(pay)

6. The check _____ at the door.
(leave)

7. The money _____ in an envelope.
(put)

EXERCISE 6   The people called to jury duty are getting instructions about what
to expect. Fill in the blanks with the passive voice of the verb in
parentheses ( ). Use the future tense.

EXAMPLE   You ___will be taken___ to a courtroom.
(take)

1. You _____ to stand up when the judge enters the room.
(tell)

2. Each of you _____ a lot of questions.
(ask)

3. The lawyers _____.
(introduce)

4. Information about the case _____ to you.
(give)

5. You _____ to eat in the courtroom.
(not/allow)

6. Twelve of you _____.
(select)

7. If you do not speak and understand English well, you

_____.
(not/pick)

8. Besides the 12 jurors, two alternates[2] _____.
(choose)

9. The rest of you _____ home.
(send)

10. All of you _____.
(pay)

[2]An *alternate* takes the place of a juror who cannot serve for some reason (such as illness).

EXERCISE 7 Fill in the blanks with the passive voice of the underlined verbs. Use the same tense.

EXAMPLE   The jury <u>took</u> a vote. The vote _____ *was taken* _____ after three hours.

1. The lawyers <u>asked</u> a lot of questions. The questions
   _____ in order to find facts.

2. The court <u>will pay</u> us. We _____ $20 a day.

3. They <u>told</u> us to wait. We _____ to wait on the second
   floor.

4. They <u>gave</u> us instructions. We _____ information
   about the law.

5. People <u>pay</u> for the services of a lawyer. Lawyers _____
   a lot of money for their services.

6. You <u>should use</u> a pen to fill out the form. A pen
   _____ for all legal documents.

7. They <u>showed</u> us a film about the court system. We
   _____ the film before we went to the courtroom.

13.4 Negatives and Questions with the Passive Voice

Compare affirmative statements to negative statements and questions with the passive voice.

SIMPLE PAST	PRESENT PERFECT
The jurors **were paid**. They **weren't paid** a lot. **Were** they **paid** in cash? No, they **weren't**. How much **were** they **paid**? Why **weren't** they **paid** in cash? Who **was paid** first?	I **have been chosen** for jury duty several times. I **haven't been chosen** this year. **Have** you ever **been chosen**? No, I **haven't**. How many times **have** you **been chosen**? Why **haven't** you **been chosen**? Which people **have been chosen**?
Language Note: Never use *do, does,* or *did* with the passive voice. *Wrong:* The juror **didn't** paid.	

EXERCISE 8 **Fill in the blanks with the negative form of the underlined verbs. Use the same tense as the underlined verbs.**

EXAMPLE I <u>was selected</u> for jury duty last year. I ___wasn't selected___ this year.

1. The jurors <u>are paid</u>. They _____ a lot of money.

2. Twelve people <u>were chosen</u>. People who don't speak English well _____.

3. Jurors <u>are allowed</u> to talk with other jurors about the case. They _____ to talk to friends and family about the case.

4. We <u>were told</u> to keep an open mind. We _____ how to vote.

5. We <u>have been given</u> instructions. We _____ our checks yet.

EXERCISE 9 **Change the statements to questions using the words in parentheses ( ).**

EXAMPLE The jurors are paid. (how much)

How much are the jurors paid? _____

1. Some people aren't selected. (why)

   _____

2. The jurors are given a lunch break. (when)

   _____

3. I wasn't chosen for the jury. (why)

   _____

4. You were given information about the case. (what kind of information)

   _____

5. A film will be shown. (when)

   _____

6. Several jurors have been sent home. (which jurors)

   _____

7. The jurors should be paid more money. (why)

   _____

8. We were told to go to the courtroom. (when)

   _____

9. The jury has been instructed by the judge. (why)

   _____

Unusual Lawsuits

Before You Read

1. Are drivers permitted to use cell phones in the area where you live?

2. Have you read about any unusual court cases in the newspaper or heard about any on TV?

CD 4, TR 14

Read the following magazine article. Pay special attention to the active and passive voice.

Did You Know?

A 2007 study by the Automobile Association of America found that 46 percent of kids aged 16 and 17 text while driving.

When a person **is injured** or **harmed**, it is the court's job to determine who is at fault. Most of these cases never **make** the news. But a few of them **appear** in the newspapers and on the evening news because they are so unusual.

In 1992, a fast-food restaurant **was sued** by a 79-year-old woman in New Mexico who **spilled** hot coffee on herself while driving. She **suffered** third-degree burns on her body. At first the woman **asked** for $11,000 to cover her medical expenses. When the restaurant **refused**, the case **went** to court and the woman **was awarded** nearly $3 million.

In 2002, a group of teenagers **sued** several fast-food chains for serving food that **made** them fat. The case **was thrown** out of court. According to Congressman Ric Keller, Americans **have to** "get away from this new culture where people always **try** to play the victim and **blame** others for their problems." Mr. Keller, who is overweight and **eats** at fast-food chains once every two weeks, **said** that suing "the food industry **is** not **going to make** a single individual any skinnier. It **will** only **make** the trial attorneys' bank accounts fatter."

In June 2004, an Indiana woman **sued** a cell phone company for causing an auto accident in which she **was involved**. The court **decided** that the manufacturer of a cell phone **cannot be held** responsible for an auto accident involving a driver using its product. In March 2000, a teenage girl in Virginia **was struck** and **killed** by a driver conducting business on a cell phone. The girl's family **sued** the driver's employer for $30 million for wrongful death. They **said** that it was the company's fault because employees **are expected** to conduct business while driving. The family **lost** its case.

We **are protected** by the law. But as individuals we **need** to take personal responsibility and not blame others for our mistakes. The court system **is designed** to protect us; it is up to us to make sure that trials **remain** serious.

13.5 Choosing Active Voice or Passive Voice

EXAMPLES	EXPLANATION
(A) A driver using a cell phone **caused** the accident. (P) The accident **was caused** by a driver using a cell phone. (A) A driver **struck** and **killed** a teenager. (P) A teenager **was struck** and **killed** by a driver.	When the sentence has a specific performer, we can use either the active (A) or passive (P) voice. The active voice puts more emphasis on the person who performs the action. The passive voice puts more emphasis on the action or the result. The performer is mentioned in a *by* phrase (*by the driver, by a woman, by the court*). The active voice is more common than the passive voice when there is a specific performer.
(P) The obesity case **was thrown** out of court. (P) The manufacturer of a cell phone **cannot be held** responsible for a car accident. (P) Some employees **are expected** to conduct business while driving.	When there is no specific performer or the performer is obvious, the passive voice is usually used.
(P) It **was found** that 80 percent of accidents are the result of driver distraction. (P) It **is believed** that cell phone use distracts drivers.	Often the passive voice is used after *it* when talking about findings, discoveries, or general beliefs.
(A) The woman **went** to court. (A) The accident **happened** in Virginia. (A) Unusual court cases **appear** in the newspaper. (A) The teenager **died**.	Some verbs have no object. We cannot make these verbs passive. Some verbs with no object are: <table><tr><td>happen</td><td>go</td><td>fall</td><td>become</td></tr><tr><td>live</td><td>sleep</td><td>come</td><td>look</td></tr><tr><td>die</td><td>seem</td><td>work</td><td>complain</td></tr><tr><td>be</td><td>remain</td><td>arrive</td><td>stay</td></tr><tr><td>appear</td><td>rain</td><td>run</td><td>sound</td></tr><tr><td>grow</td><td>depend</td><td>laugh</td><td>leave (a place)</td></tr></table>
(A) **She** sued **them**. (P) **They** were sued by **her**. (A) **He** helps **us**. (P) **We** are helped by **him**.	Notice the difference in pronouns in an active sentence and a passive sentence. After *by*, the object pronoun is used.

Language Note: Even though *have* and *want* are followed by an object, these verbs are not usually used in the passive voice.

He **has** a cell phone. (*Not:* A cell phone is had by him.)

She **wants** a new car. (*Not:* A new car is wanted by her.)

EXERCISE 10 Change these sentences from active to passive voice. Mention the performer in a *by* phrase. Use the same tense as the underlined verbs.

EXAMPLE An Indiana woman <u>sued</u> a cell phone company.
A cell phone company was sued by an Indiana woman.

1. Employees <u>use</u> cell phones.

_____

2. A driver <u>hit</u> a pedestrian.

_____

3. The court <u>threw out</u> the case.

_____

4. Distracted drivers <u>cause</u> accidents.

_____

5. Congress <u>makes</u> the laws.

_____

6. <u>Should</u> the government <u>control</u> cell phone use?

_____

7. The president <u>signs</u> new laws.

_____

8. The court <u>has decided</u> the case.

_____

9. The judge <u>will make</u> a decision.

_____

10. Fast-food restaurants <u>sell</u> hamburgers and fries.

_____

EXERCISE 11 The following sentences would be better in passive voice without a performer. Change them to passive voice. Use the same tense as the underlined verbs.

EXAMPLE They <u>paid</u> me for jury duty.
I was paid for jury duty.

1. They <u>sent</u> me a questionnaire.

_____

2. They <u>have taken</u> us to a separate room.

_____

3. They <u>told</u> us not to discuss the case.

_____

4. They <u>will choose</u> 12 people.

_____

5. <u>Has</u> someone <u>selected</u> your name?

_____

6. They <u>didn't permit</u> us to read any newspapers.

_____

7. They <u>will not select</u> him again for jury duty.

_____

8. <u>Will</u> they <u>pay</u> you?

_____

9. They <u>don't allow</u> us to eat in the courtroom.

_____

10. Someone <u>has called</u> my name.

_____

EXERCISE 12 **The following sentences would be better in active voice. Change them to active voice. Use the same tense as the underlined verbs.**

EXAMPLE Fast food <u>is eaten</u> by Mr. Keller.
Mr. Keller eats fast food.

1. A cell phone <u>was had</u> by the driver.

_____

2. Hot coffee <u>was spilled</u> by the driver.

_____

3. <u>Is</u> a cell phone <u>used</u> by you?

_____

4. The car <u>has been driven</u> by me.

_____

5. A lot of money <u>is made</u> by lawyers.

_____

6. An earpiece <u>should be used</u> by drivers with cell phones.

_____

7. Business <u>is conducted</u> by me from my car.

_____

8. The news <u>is watched</u> by us every night.

_____

9. Fast food <u>is eaten</u> by a lot of teenagers.

_____

10. The accident <u>will be reported</u> by them.

_____

EXERCISE **13** **Fill in the blanks with the active or passive voice of the verb in parentheses ( ). Use the tense or modal given.**

🔊
CD 4, TR 15

In more than 50 countries, laws __**have been passed**__ that prohibit
(_example: present perfect: pass_)
drivers from using cell phones. In a few countries, such as Japan, both

hand-held and hands-free cell phone use _____.
(_1 present: ban_)
In the U.S., the law _____ on the place where you
(_2 present: depend_)
_____. In New York, for example, the use of
(_3 present: live_)
hand-held cell phones while driving _____, but
(_4 present: prohibit_)
the use of hands-free units _____. A driver who
(_5 present: permit_)
_____ this law can be fined $100 for a first offense,
(_6 present: not/obey_)
$200 for a second, and $500 after that. More and more states

_____ to become tougher on drivers who use
(_7 present perfect: start_)
cell phones.

Texting while driving _____ an even greater problem.
(_8 present perfect: become_)
Drivers _____ to look away from the road in order to text.
(_9 present: need_)
The risk of causing an accident while texting is 15 times higher than it is while

using a cell phone. In New York, drivers who text _____
(_10 future: punish_)
with a fine of up to $150. In Utah, drivers who text and cause a serious

accident _____ to jail for up to 15 years.
(_11 can/send_)
But the problem of driver distraction is not only a result of cell phones

and texting. According to one study conducted, it was found that 80 percent

of accidents _____ by drivers who are not paying attention.
(_12 present: cause_)
This study _____ that drivers _____ by
(_13 past: determine_)   (_14 present: distract_)
many things: eating, putting on makeup, reading, reaching for things, and

changing stations on the radio. It is clear that all drivers

_____ to give driving their full attention.
(15 present: need)

EXERCISE **14** **Fill in the blanks with the passive or active voice of the verb in parentheses ( ), using the past tense.**

🔊
CD 4, TR 16

A: Why weren't you at work last week? Were you sick?

B: No. I _____**was chosen**_____ to be on a jury.
(example: choose)

A: How was it?

B: It was very interesting. A man _____
(1 arrest)

for fighting with a police officer.

A: Oh. How was the jury selection process?

B: The jury selection was interesting too. But it took

half a day to choose 12 people.

A: Why?

B: The judge and lawyers _____ more than 50 people.
(2 interview)

A: Why so many people?

B: Well, several people _____ the judge's questions.
(3 not/understand)

They _____ English very well. And a
(4 not/speak)

woman _____ the judge that she was very sick.
(5 tell)

The judge _____ her permission to leave. I don't
(6 give)

know why the other people _____.
(7 not/choose)

A: What kind of questions _____ by the
(8 you/ask)

judge and lawyers?

B: First the lawyers _____ to see if we could be fair.
(9 want)

Some jurors _____ that they had a bad experience
(10 say)

with a police officer. Those jurors _____.
(11 not/select)

A: Why not?

B: Because the judge probably thought they couldn't be fair in this case.

A: How long did the trial last?

B: Only two days.

(*continued*)

A: _____ about the case with your family when
  (12 you/talk)

you _____ home the first night?
  (13 go)

B: Oh, no. We _____ not to talk to anyone about the
  (14 tell)

case. When it was over, I _____ my wife and kids
  (15 tell)

about it.

A: How long did it take the jurors to make a decision?

B: About two hours. One of the jurors _____
  (16 not/agree)

with the other 11 jurors. We _____ about the
  (17 talk)

evidence until she changed her mind.

A: _____ you for the days you missed work?
  (18 your boss/pay)

B: Of course. He had to pay me. That's the law.

A: Now that you've done it once, you won't have to do it again. Right?

B: That's not true. This was the second time I _____.
  (19 choose)

Summary of Lesson 13

Active and Passive Voice—Forms	
ACTIVE	**PASSIVE**
He **drove** the car.	The car **was driven** by him.
He **didn't drive** the car.	The car **wasn't driven** by him.
He **will drive** the car.	The car **will be driven** by him.
He **has driven** the car.	The car **has been driven** by him.
He often **drives** the car.	The car **is** often **driven** by him.
He **should drive** the car.	The car **should be driven** by him.
Did he **drive** the car?	**Was** the car **driven** by him?
When **did** he **drive** the car?	When **was** the car **driven** by him?
Which car **did** he **drive**?	Which car **was driven** by him?

The Active Voice—Use	
EXAMPLES	**EXPLANATION**
I **bought** a new cell phone. He **eats** fast food. We **will drive** the car.	In most cases, the active voice is used when there is a choice between active and passive.
The accident **happened** last month. She **went** to court.	When there is no object, the active voice must be used. There is no choice.

The Passive Voice—Use

EXAMPLES	EXPLANATION
I **was chosen** for jury duty. My cell phone **was made** in Japan.	Use the passive voice when the performer is not known or is not important.
The criminal **was taken** to jail. Some employees **are expected** to conduct business while driving.	Use the passive voice when the performer is obvious.
Cell phones **are used** all over the world. Jury duty **is considered** a responsibility of every citizen.	Use the passive voice when the performer is everybody or people in general.
The court paid me. I **was paid** at the end of the day. The coffee was very hot. The coffee **was bought** at a fast-food restaurant.	Use the passive voice when the emphasis is shifted from the performer to the receiver of the action.
It **was discovered** that many accidents are the result of driver distraction. It **is believed** that a person can get a fair trial in the U.S.	Use the passive voice with *it* when talking about findings, discoveries, or beliefs.
Accidents **are caused** by distracted drivers. A fast-food company **was sued** by a woman in New Mexico.	Use the passive voice when the emphasis is on the receiver of the action more than on the performer. (In this case, the performer is included in a *by* phrase.)

Editing Advice

1. Never use *do*, *does*, or *did* with the passive voice.

   wasn't found
   The money ~~didn't find~~.

   were
   Where ~~did~~ the jurors taken?

2. Don't use the passive voice with *happen*, *die*, *become*, *sleep*, *work*, *live*, *fall*, *seem*, or other verbs with no object.

   My grandfather ~~was~~ died four years ago.

3. Don't confuse the *-ing* form with the past participle.

   taken
   The criminal was ~~taking~~ to jail.

4. Don't forget the *-ed* ending for a regular past participle.

                        ed

    My cousin was select˰ to be on a jury.

5. Don't forget to use *be* with a passive sentence.

             were

    The books˰found on the floor by the janitor.

6. Use the correct word order with adverbs.

    I was told (never) about the problem.

Editing Quiz

Some of the shaded words and phrases have mistakes. Find the mistakes and correct them. If the shaded words are correct, write *C*.

            C

A: You didn't come to class all last week. What ~~was~~ happened? Were you sick?
      (example)   *(example)*

B: No. I had jury duty.
     (1)

A: But you're not a citizen, are you?

B: Yes, I am. I was become a citizen six months ago. Last month, I received a
                (2)   *(3)*

    letter in the mail telling me I had to report for duty.

A: Did you selected for a jury? You're still an ESL student!
     (4)   *(5)*

B: Yes. I was selected. My English is far from perfect, but I was ask a lot of
          (6)   *(7)*

    questions by the judge and I answered them without a problem. Anyway,
                               (8)

    I was surprised that I chosen.
               (9)

A: Was it an interesting case?

B: Not really. It was about a traffic accident. A man hit a woman's car and
                                            (10)

    he left the scene of the accident. Her car was badly damage.
      (11)   *(12)*

A: Did the woman injured?
       (13)

B: She had back pain and had to go for physical therapy.

A: How did the driver caught?
(14)   (15)

B: The woman saw his license plate and wrote down the number.
(16)   (17)

A: Then what was happened?
(18)

B: She called the police and they caught him. He was taking to the police
(19)   (20)

station. He was driven without a license. Also, he was talking on a cell
(21)   (22)

phone while he was driving. It's not permitted to do that in this city.
(23)

A: I didn't know that. I was told never about that rule.
(24)

B: Well, now you know!

Lesson 13 Test/Review

PART 1   **Change sentences from active to passive voice. Do not mention the performer. (The performer is in parentheses.) Use the same tense as the underlined verb.**

EXAMPLE   (Someone) took my dictionary.
              My dictionary was taken. _____

1. (People) speak English in the U.S.

   _____

2. (You) can use a dictionary during the test.

   _____

3. (The police) took the criminal to jail.

   _____

4. (People) have seen the president on TV many times.

   _____

5. (Someone) will take you to the courtroom.

   _____

6. (Someone) has broken the mirror into small pieces.

   _____

7. (People) <u>expect</u> you to learn English in the U.S.

_____

8. (They) <u>don't allow</u> cameras in the courtroom.

_____

PART 2 **Change the sentences from passive to active voice. Use the same tense as the underlined verb.**

EXAMPLE You <u>were told</u> by me to bring your books.
I told you to bring your books. _____

1. You <u>have been told</u> by the teacher to write a composition.

_____

2. Your phone bill <u>must be paid</u>.

_____

3. You <u>are not allowed</u> by the teacher to use your books during a test.

_____

4. The tests <u>will be returned</u> by the teacher.

_____

5. When <u>are</u> wedding gifts <u>opened</u> by the bride and groom?

_____

6. Your missing car <u>was not found</u> by the police.

_____

PART 3 **Fill in the blanks with the passive or active form of the verb in parentheses ( ). Use an appropriate tense or the modal given.**

EXAMPLES The tests _____**will be returned**_____ tomorrow.
(will/return)

The teacher _____**will return**_____ the tests.
(will/return)

1. My neighbor had a heart attack and _____ to the
(take)

hospital in an ambulance yesterday.

2. I _____ my neighbor in the hospital tomorrow.
(will/visit)

3. I _____ the movie _Star Wars_ five times.
(see)

4. This movie _____ by millions of people.
   (see)

5. I _____ a lot of friends.
   (have)

6. I _____ many times by my friends.
   (help)

7. Ten people _____ in the fire last night.
   (die)

8. Five people _____ by the fire department in
   (rescue)

   yesterday's fire.

9. Her husband _____ home from work at 6 P.M.
   (come)

   every day.

10. He _____ home by his coworker last night.
    (drive)

11. The answer to your question _____ by anyone.
    (not/know)

12. Even the teacher _____ the answer to your question.
    (not/know)

Expansion

Classroom
Activities

❶ Form a small group and talk about the legal system in another country. Use the chart below to get ideas.

Country: _____

	Yes	No
People are treated fairly in court.		
Citizens are selected to be on a jury.		
People are represented by lawyers in court.		
Lawyers make a lot of money.		
Famous trials are shown on TV.		
Punishment is severe for certain crimes.		
The death penalty is used in some cases.		
The laws are fair.		

❷ Form two groups. One group will make a presentation telling why cell phone use should be permitted in cars. One group will make a presentation telling why cell phone use should *not* be permitted in cars.

Talk

About It

1 Would you like to be on a jury? Why or why not?

2 In a small group, discuss your impressions of the American legal system from what you've seen on TV, from what you've read, or from your own experience.

3 Do you think drivers who talk on cell phones or text while driving cause accidents?

4 What laws should be changed in the U.S.? What laws should be added?

Write

About It

1 Write about an experience you have had with the court system in the U.S. or your native country.

2 Write about a famous court case that you know of. Do you agree with the decision of the jury?

A Famous Court Case

I read about an interesting court case involving the governor of Illinois, George Ryan. He was convicted in 2006 of corruption while in office. He illegally gave out driver's licenses to unqualified truck drivers. A family was killed by one of these drivers...

 For more practice using grammar in context, please visit our Web site.

Grammar
Articles

Other/Another

Indefinite Pronouns

Context
Money

Articles precede nouns and tell whether a noun is definite or indefinite.

EXAMPLES	EXPLANATION
Do you have **a credit card**? I bought **an old house**.	The indefinite articles are *a* and *an*.
It's a holiday today. **The banks** are closed. There are many poor people in **the world**.	The definite article is *the*.
Money is important for everyone. **Teenagers** like to spend money.	Sometimes a noun is used without an article.

Kids and Money

Before You Read

1. Do you think parents should give money to their children? At what age?

2. Do you think teenagers should work while they're in high school?

CD 4, TR 17

Read the following magazine article. Pay special attention to nouns and the articles that precede them. (Some nouns have no article.)

Kids in the U.S. like to spend **money**. In 2009, the average 17-year-old spent more than $100 a week. Much of today's **advertising** is directed at **kids.** When you go into **a store**, you often hear **toddlers**,[1] who are

¹A *toddler* is a child between the ages of one and three.

just learning to talk, saying to their **parents**, "Buy me **a toy**. Buy me **some candy**." **Some kids** feel **gratitude** when they receive **a dollar** or **a toy** from **a grandparent**. But some **kids** feel **a sense** of **entitlement**[2]. Even during **the** hard economic **times** of the early 1990s, **sales** of **soft drinks, designer jeans, fast food, sneakers, gum,** and **dolls** remained high. **One factor** in parents' **generosity** is **guilt**. As **parents** become busier in their **jobs**, they often feel guilty about not spending **time** with their **kids**. Often they deal with their **guilt** by giving their **kids money** and **gifts**.

To help **children** understand **the value** of **money**, **parents** often give their **children an allowance**. **The** child's **spending** is limited to **the money** he or she receives each week. How much should **parents** give **a child** as **an allowance**? **Some parents** give **the child a dollar** for each year of his or her age. **A** five-year-old would get five dollars. **A** fifteen-year-old would get fifteen dollars. **Some parents** pay their **kids** extra for **chores**, such as taking out **the garbage** or shoveling **snow**. Other **parents** believe **kids** should do **chores** as part of their family **responsibilities**.

When is **the** right **time** to start talking to **kids** about **money**? According to Nathan Dungan, a financial **expert, the** right **time** is as soon as **kids** can say, "I want." By **the time** they start **school**, they must know there are **limits**.

14.2 The Indefinite Article—Classifying or Identifying the Subject

EXAMPLES	EXPLANATION
A doll is **a toy**. A toddler is **a small child**. A penny is **a one-cent coin**. "Inflation" is **an economic term**.	After the verb *be*, we use the indefinite articles *a* or *an* + singular count noun to define or classify the subject of the sentence. Singular subject + *is* + *a(n)* + (adjective) + noun
Guilt is **an emotion**. Generosity is **a good quality**.	We can classify a noncount subject: Noncount subject + *is* + *a(n)* + (adjective) + noun
Jeans are **popular clothes**. Teenagers are **young adults**. Chores are **everyday jobs**.	When we classify or define a plural subject, we don't use an article. Plural subject + *are* + (adjective) + noun

Language Note: We can also use *be* in the past tense to give a definition.
    The Depression **was** a difficult time in American history.
    Abraham Lincoln **was** an American president.

[2]A sense of *entitlement* is a feeling that you have the right to receive something.

EXERCISE 1 Define the following words. Answers may vary.

EXAMPLE A toddler ___is a small child.___

1. A teenager _____
2. A quarter _____
3. A dime _____
4. A credit card _____
5. A wallet _____
6. Gold _____
7. Silver and gold _____

EXERCISE 2 Tell who these people are or were by classifying them. These people were mentioned in previous lessons in this book. Answers will vary.

EXAMPLE Martin Luther King, Jr. ___was an African-American leader.___

1. Albert Einstein _____
2. Tiger Woods _____
3. Erik Weihenmayer _____
4. Barack Obama _____
5. George Dawson _____
6. Navajos _____

14.3 The Indefinite Article—Introducing a Noun

EXAMPLES	EXPLANATION
She has **a son.** Her son has **a job.** Her son has **a checking account.**	Use *a* or *an* to introduce a singular noun.
He has (**some**) toys. He doesn't have (**any**) video games. Does he have (**any**) CDs?	Use *some* and *any* to introduce a plural noun. *Some* and *any* can be omitted.
He has (**some**) money. He doesn't have (**any**) cash. Does he have (**any**) time?	Use *some* and *any* to introduce a noncount noun. *Some* and *any* can be omitted.
Language Notes: 1. *Some* is used in affirmative statements. 2. *Any* is used in negative statements. 3. Both *some* and *any* can be used in questions.	

EXERCISE 3   **Fill in the blanks with the correct word: *a, an, some,* or *any*.**

EXAMPLE   There are ____*some*____ symbols on the back of a credit card.

1. Do you have _____ account with the bank?
2. Do you have _____ money in your savings account?
3. I have _____ twenty-dollar bill in my pocket.
4. I have _____ quarters in my pocket.
5. I have _____ money with me.
6. Do you have _____ credit cards?
7. I don't have _____ change.
8. Buy me _____ toy.
9. Buy me _____ candy.
10. I need _____ dollar.
11. Many teenagers want to have _____ job.
12. Does your little brother get _____ allowance?

EXERCISE 4   **A mother (M) and a son (S) are talking. Fill in the blanks with *a, an, some,* or *any*.**

🔊

CD 4, TR 18

S: I want to get ____*a*____ job.
                (example)

M: But you're only 16 years old.

S: I'm old enough to work. I need to

make _____ money.
     (1)

M: But we give you _____ allowance each
                 (2)

week. Isn't that enough money for you?

S: You only give me $15 a week. That's not even enough to buy

_____ CD or take _____ girl to _____ movie.
  (3)   (4)   (5)

M: If you work, what are you going to do about school? You won't have

_____ time to study. Do you know how hard it is to
  (6)

work and do well in school?

S: Of course, I do. You know I'm _____ good student.
                               (7)

I'm sure I won't have _____ problems working part-time.
                      (8)

M: Well, I'm worried about your grades falling. Maybe we should raise

your allowance. That way you won't have to work.   (*continued*)

S: I want to have my own money. I want to buy _____ new clothes.
(9)

And I'm going to save money to buy _____ car someday.
(10)

M: Why do you want a car? You have _____ bike.
(11)

S: Bikes are great for exercise, but if my job is far away, I'll need a car for transportation.

M: So, you need _____ job to buy _____ car, and you need
(12)   (13)

_____ car to get to work.
(14)

S: Yes. You know, a lot of my friends work, and they're good students.

M: Well, let me think about it.

S: Mom, I'm not _____ baby anymore. I need _____ job.
(15)   (16)

14.4 The Definite Article

We use *the* to talk about a specific person or thing or a unique person or thing.

EXAMPLES	EXPLANATION
The book talks about kids and money. **The author** wants to teach kids to be responsible with money.	The sentences to the left refer to a specific object or person that is present. There is no other book or author present, so the listener knows which noun is referred to.
Many kids in **the world** are poor. **The first** chapter talks about small children. **The back** of the book has information about the author. When is **the right** time to talk to kids about money?	Sometimes there is only one of something. There is only one world, only one first chapter, only one back of a book. We use *the* with the following words: *first, second, next, last, only, same,* and *right.*
Where's **the** teacher? I have a question about **the** homework.	When students in the same class talk about **the** teacher, **the** textbook, **the** homework, **the** board, they are talking about a specific one that they share.
Did you read **the article about money**? Children often spend **the money they get from their grandparents**.	The sentences to the left refer to a specific noun that is defined in the phrase or clause after the noun: *the article **about money**; the money **they get from their grandparents**.*

EXAMPLES	EXPLANATION
I'm going to **the** store after work. Do you need anything? **The** bank is closed. I'll go tomorrow. You should make an appointment with **the** doctor.	We often use *the* with certain familiar places and people when we refer to the one that we usually use: the bank the beach the bus the zoo the post office the train the park the doctor the movies the store
a. I saw **a child** in the supermarket with her mother. b. **The child** kept saying, "Buy me this, buy me that." a. The mother bought **some toys**. b. She paid for **the toys** with her credit card. a. The teenager saved **some money**. b. She used **the money** to buy new clothes.	a. A singular noun is first introduced with *a* or *an*. A plural noun or noncount noun is first introduced with *some*. b. When referring to the same noun again, the definite article *the* is used.
My grandparents gave me lots of presents. **Kim's kids** have lots of toys.	Don't use the definite article with a possessive form. *Wrong:* My the grandparents *Wrong:* Kim's the kids

EXERCISE **5** Fill in the blanks with *the, a, an, any,* or *some.*

Conversation 1: **between two friends**

CD 4, TR 19

A: Where are you going?

B: To _____**the**_____ bank. I want to
       (example)
deposit _____ check.
       (1)

A: _____ bank is probably closed
   (2)
now.

B: No problem. I have _____ ATM card. There's _____
         (3)   *(4)*
ATM on _____ corner of Wilson and Sheridan.
     (5)

A: I'll go with you. I want to get _____ cash.
                           (6)

(*Later, at the ATM*)

B: Oh, no. _____ ATM is out of order.
        (7)

A: Don't worry. There's _____ ATM in _____ supermarket
              (8)   *(9)*
near my house.

(*continued*)

Conversation 2: between two students (A and B) at the same school

A: Is there _____ cafeteria at this school?
(1)

B: Yes, there is. It's on _____ first floor of this building.
(2)

A: I want to buy _____ cup of coffee.
(3)

B: You don't have to go to _____ cafeteria. There's _____
(4) (5)
coffee machine on this floor.

A: I only have a one-dollar bill. Do you have _____ change?
(6)

B: There's _____ dollar-bill changer next to _____
(7) (8)
coffee machine.

Conversation 3: between two students in the same class

A: Where's _____ teacher? It's already 7:00.
(1)

B: Maybe she's absent today.

A: I'll go to _____ English office and ask if anyone knows where
(2)
she is.

B: That's _____ good idea.
(3)

(*A few minutes later*)

A: I talked to _____ secretary in _____ English office. She said
(4) (5)
that _____ teacher just called. She's going to be about 15 minutes
(6)
late. She had _____ problem with her car.
(7)

14.5 Making Generalizations

When we make a generalization, we say that something is true of ALL members of a group.

EXAMPLES	EXPLANATION
a. **Children** like to copy their friends. b. **A child** likes to copy his or her friends. a. **Video games** are expensive. b. **A video game** is expensive.	There are two ways to make a generalization about a countable subject: a. Use no article + plural noun. OR b. Use *a* or *an* + singular noun.
Money doesn't buy happiness. **Love** is more important than money. **Honesty** is a good quality.	To make a generalization about a noncount subject, don't use an article.
a. Children like **toys**. a. People like to use **credit cards**. b. Everyone needs **money**. b. No one has enough **time**.	Don't use an article to make a generalization about the object of the sentence. a. Use the plural form for count nouns. b. Noncount nouns are always singular.

Language Note: Do not use *some* or *any* with generalizations.
Compare:
    I need **some money** to buy a new bike.
    Everyone needs **money**.

EXERCISE **6** Decide if the statement is general (true of all examples of the subject), or specific (true of the pictures on these pages or of specific objects that everyone in the class can agree on). Fill in the blanks with *a*, *an*, *the*, or *Ø* (for no article).

EXAMPLES   ___Ø___ ^Cchildren like ___Ø___ toys.

     ___The___ toys are broken.

1. _____ American teenager likes to have a job.

2. _____ teenager is shoveling snow to make money.

3. _____ teenagers like _____ cars.

4. _____ jeans are popular.

5. _____ jeans are torn.

6. _____ money is important for everyone.

7. _____ money on the table is mine.

8. Do you like _____ kids?

9. _____ American kids like to spend money.

10. _____ child is saying to her mother, "I want."

11. Do you like to use _____ credit cards?

12. _____ credit card and the wallet are mine.

13. _____ textbooks at American colleges aren't free.

14. _____ textbook on the table costs $39.99.

15. Where did you buy _____ textbooks for your courses?

EXERCISE 7 **ABOUT YOU** Tell if you like the following or not. For count nouns (C), use the plural form. For noncount nouns (NC), use the singular form.

EXAMPLES coffee (NC)   apple (C)
I like coffee.   I don't like apples.

1. tea (NC)   **4.** potato chip (C)   **7.** cookie (C)

2. corn (NC)   **5.** milk (NC)   **8.** pizza (NC)

3. peach (C)   **6.** orange (C)   **9.** potato (C)

EXERCISE 8 Fill in the blanks with *the, a, an, some, any,* or *Ø* (for no article). In some cases, more than one answer is possible.

CD 4, TR 20

A: Where are you going?

B: I'm going to ___the___ post office. I need to buy _____ stamps.
    (example)   (1)

A: I'll go with you. I want to mail _____ package to my parents.
                                       (2)

B: What's in _____ package?
                (3)

A: _____ shirts for my father, _____ coat for my sister,
       (4)   (5)

    and _____ money for my mother.
        (6)

B: You should never send _____ money by mail.
                            (7)

A: I know. My mother never received _____ money that I sent in my
                                        (8)

    last letter. But what can I do? I don't have _____ checking account.
                                                 (9)

B: You can buy _____ money order at _____ bank.
                  (10)   (11)

A: How much does it cost?

B: Well, if you have _____ account in _____ bank, it's
                        (12)   (13)

    usually free. If not, you'll probably have to pay a fee.

A: What about _____ currency exchange on Wright Street? Do
                 (14)

    they sell _____ money orders?
              (15)

B: Yes.

A: Why don't we go there? We can save _____ time. It's on
(16)

_____ same street as _____ post office.
(17) (18)

EXERCISE **9** **Two women are talking. Fill in the blanks with *the*, *a*, *an*, *some*, or Ø (for no article). Answers may vary.**

CD 4, TR 21

A: I bought my daughter _____*a*_____ new doll for her birthday. She's
(example)

been asking me to buy it for her for two months. But she played with

_____ doll for about three days and then lost interest.
(1)

B: That's how _____ kids are. They don't understand
(2)

_____ value of money.
(3)

A: You're right. They think that _____ money grows
(4)

on _____ trees.
(5)

B: I suppose it's our fault. We have to set _____ good example. We
(6)

buy a lot of things we don't really need. We use _____ credit
(7)

cards instead of _____ cash and worry about paying the bill later.
(8)

A: I suppose you're right. Last month we bought _____ new
(9)

flat-screen TV. We were at the store looking for a DVD player when we

saw it. It's so much nicer than our old TV, so we decided to get it and

put our _____ old TV in _____ basement. I suppose
(10) (11)

we didn't really need it.

B: Last weekend my husband bought _____ new CD
(12)

player. And he bought _____ new CDs. I asked him what
(13)

was wrong with our old CD player, and he said that it played only

two CDs at a time. _____ new CD player has room for ten CDs.
(14)

A: Well, when we complain about our kids, we should realize that they

are imitating us.

B: We need to make _____ changes in our own behavior. I'm
(15)

going to start _____ budget tonight. I'm going to start saving
(16)

_____ money each month.
(17)

A: Me too.

Articles; *Other/Another*; Indefinite Pronouns   **447**

14.6 General or Specific with Quantity Words

If we put *of the* after a quantity word (*all, most, some,* etc.), we are referring to something specific. Without *of the*, the noun is general.

EXAMPLES	EXPLANATION
General: **All** children like toys. **Most** American homes have a television. **Many** teenagers have jobs. **Some** people are very rich. **Very few** people are billionaires.	We use *all, most, many, some, (a) few,* and *(a) little* before general nouns.

Specific:
All (of) the students in this class have a textbook.
Most of the students in my art class have talent.
Many of the topics in this book are about life in America.
Some of the people in my building come from Haiti.
Very few of the students in this class are American citizens.
Very little of the time spent in this class is used for reading.
None of the classrooms at this school has a telephone.
	We use *all of the, most of the, many of the, some of the, (a) few of the, (a) little of the,* and *none of the* before specific nouns.
	After *all, of* is often omitted.
	    All the students in this class have a textbook.
	After *none of the* + plural noun, a singular verb is correct. However, you will often hear a plural verb used.
	    None of the classrooms **have** a telephone.

Language Note: Remember there is a difference between *a few* and *(very) few*, *a little*, and *(very) little*. When we omit ***a***, the emphasis is on the negative. We are saying the quantity is not enough. (See Lesson 5, Section 5.14 for more information.)
    Few people wanted to have a party. The party was canceled.
    A few people came to the meeting. We discussed our plans.

EXERCISE **10** Fill in the blanks with *all, most, some,* or *(very) few* to make a general statement about Americans. Discuss your answers.

EXAMPLE   ___Most___ Americans have a car.

1. _____ Americans have educational opportunities.

2. _____ Americans have a TV.

3. _____ American families have more than eight children.

4. _____ Americans know where my native country is.

5. _____ Americans shake hands when they meet.

6. _____ Americans use credit cards.

7. _____ Americans are natives of America.

8. _____ American citizens can vote.

9. _____ Americans speak my native language.

10. _____ Americans are unfriendly to me.

EXERCISE **11** **ABOUT YOU** **Fill in the blanks with a quantity word to make a true statement about specific nouns. If you use *none*, change the verb to the singular form.**

EXAMPLES   ___*All of the*___ students in this class want to learn English.

    ___*None of the students*___ in this class come^s from Australia.

1. _____ students in this class speak Spanish.

2. _____ students brought their books to class today.

3. _____ students are absent today.

4. _____ students want to learn English.

5. _____ students have jobs.

6. _____ students are married.

7. _____ students are going to return to their native countries.

8. _____ lessons in this book end with a review.

9. _____ pages in this book have pictures.

10. _____ tests in this class are hard.

Bills, Bills, Bills

Before
You Read

1. How many bills a month do you get?

2. How do you pay your bills? By check? By credit card? Online?

CD 4, TR 22

Read the following conversation. Pay special attention to *other* and *another*.

(continued)

A: Last month I went to the doctor, and she sent me to get an X-ray. I got a bill and paid it, but then I got **another one**. Can you help me figure this out?

B: Let's see. Well, one bill is from the doctor. **The other one** is from the X-ray lab.

A: This is crazy. Why don't they send just one bill?

B: That's how it is in the U.S.

A: And look how high the bill is. I had one test and it cost over $600.

B: Do you have insurance?

A: Yes.

B: Wait for your insurance to pay. After your insurance pays, they'll send you **another** bill that shows the amount you have to pay.

A: There are two phone numbers. Which one should I call?

B: The first number is for telephone service. **The other** number is a fax number.

A: How do I pay? Can I send cash?

B: Never send cash by mail. There are two methods of payment: One method is by check. **The other** is by credit card.

A: I hate paying bills. Every month I get a gas bill, a cell phone bill, an electricity bill, a cable bill, and **others**. This is so confusing.

B: Some people pay by check. But **others** set up direct payment. Call the electric company and all **the others** to see if you can do a direct debit[3]. That way you don't have to think about bills every month.

[3]A *direct debit* means the money goes straight from your checking account to pay the bill.

14.7 *Another* and *Other*

The use of *other* and *another* depends on whether a noun is singular or plural, definite or indefinite.

The other + a singular noun is definite. It means the only one remaining.

There are two numbers.   X   ⊗

One number is the phone number. ⟶

The other number is the fax number. ⟶

The other + a plural noun is definite. It means all the remaining ones.

                                           X   ⟨X X X X X⟩

Call the electric company. ⟶

Call all **the other** companies. ⟶

Another + a singular noun is indefinite. It means one of several.

                                           X   X X ⓧ X X

One bill is from the electric company. ⟶

Another bill is from the gas company. ⟶

Other + a plural noun is indefinite. It means some, but not all, of the remaining ones.

                                           X   X ⟨X X⟩ X X

Some people pay by check. ⟶

Other people pay by credit. ⟶

DR. MARY THOMPSON, M.D.
20 BAKER ST. PHOENIX, AZ 85003
PH: (602) 555-1215 FAX: (602) 555-1213
CONSULTATION BY APPOINTMENT

DATE: _____3/14/10_____

Morgan Sweet
20 Maple Rd.
Phoenix, AZ 85003

FOR PROFESSIONAL SERVICES

office visit	$40.00
blood test	$150.00
radiology	$410.00

TOTAL DUE: _____$600.00_____

PAYMENT RECEIVED: _____

14.8 More About *Another* and *Other*

EXAMPLES	EXPLANATION
One number is the phone number. The other **one** is the fax number. Call the electric company. Call the other **ones** too.	We can use the pronouns *one* or *ones* in place of the noun. For plurals, put the **s** on *one*, not on *other*. *Wrong:* the other<u>s</u> ones
Some people pay by check. **Others** pay by credit card.	When the plural noun or pronoun (*ones*) is omitted, change *other* to *others*.
I have two bank accounts. One is for savings. **My other** account is for checking.	*The* is omitted when we use a possessive form. *Wrong:* My *the* other account is for checking.
I'm busy paying bills now. Can we talk **another** time? Can we talk **any other** time? Can we talk **some other** time?	After *some* or *any*, *another* is changed to *other*. *Wrong:* Can you come *any* another time?
After your insurance pays, your doctor will send you **another** bill. I received one doctor bill. Then I received **another** one.	*Another* is sometimes used to mean a different one, or one more.

EXERCISE 12   **Fill in the blanks with *the other, another, the others, others,* or *other*.**

EXAMPLE   I have a question about my doctor bill. I have ___another___ one about my light bill.

1. I have one more bill to pay this month. I paid all _____ bills.

2. I received one bill for the X-ray. Then I received _____ one.

3. The doctor gave me two tests. One test was an X-ray. _____ one was a blood test.

4. One side of the credit card has a name and number. _____ side has a place to sign your name.

5. If I use the ATM at my bank, I don't have to pay a fee. If I use it at any _____ bank, I have to pay a fee.

6. The bank is going to close now. Please come back some _____ time.

7. *Money* is a noncount noun. _____ ones are *love, freedom,* and *time.*

8. Some kids get an allowance for doing nothing. _____ have to do chores to get an allowance. But not all kids get an allowance.

9. The child gets presents from his grandparents. One grandparent died, but _____ three are alive.

10. The child has a lot of toys, but he wants _____ one.

EXERCISE 13   **A grandson (GS) and grandfather (GF) are talking. Fill in the blanks with *the other, another, the others,* or *other.***

🔊
CD 4, TR 23

GS: I want to buy ___another___ pair of sneakers.
                            (example)

GF: What?! You already have about six pairs of sneakers. In fact,

      I bought you a new pair last month for your birthday.

GS: The new pair is fine, but _____ five are too small
                                (1)

      for me. You know I'm growing very fast, so I threw them away.

GF: Why did you throw them away? _____ boys
                                     (2)

      in your neighborhood could use them.

GS: They wouldn't like them. They're out of style.

GF: You kids are so wasteful today. What's wrong with

      the sneakers I bought you last month? If they fit you, why

      do you need _____ pair?
                      (3)

GS: Everybody in my class at school has red sneakers with the

      laces tied backward. The sneakers you gave me are not in style

      anymore.

GF: Do you always have to have what all _____ kids in
                                      (4)

      school have? Can't you think for yourself?

GS: Didn't you ask your parents for stuff when you were in junior high?

GF: My parents were poor, and my two brothers and I worked to help

      them. When we couldn't wear our clothes anymore because we

      outgrew them, we gave them to _____ families nearby.
                                        (5)

      And our neighbors gave us the things that their children outgrew.

      One neighbor had two sons. One son was a year older

      than me. _____ one was two years younger. So we
                    (6)

      were constantly passing clothes back and forth.

GS: What about style? When clothes went out of style, didn't you throw

      them out?

(continued)

Articles; *Other/Another*; Indefinite Pronouns   **453**

GF: No. We never threw things out. Styles were not as important to us then. We didn't waste our parents' money thinking of styles. In fact, my oldest brother worked in a factory and gave all his salary to our parents. My _____ brother and I helped our father in his
(7)
business. My dad didn't give us a salary or an allowance. It was our duty to help him.

GS: You don't understand how important it is to look like all

_____ kids.
(8)

GF: I guess I don't. I'm old-fashioned. Every generation has

_____ way of looking at things.
(9)

The High Cost of a College Education

Before You Read

1. Have you received any financial aid to take this course?

2. Do you know how much it costs to get a college degree in the U.S.?

CD 4, TR 24

Read the following conversation between a son (S) and a dad (D) and the Web article that follows. Pay attention to *one*, *some*, *any* (indefinite pronouns), and *it* and *them* (definite pronouns).

S: I decided not to go to college, Dad.

D: What? Do you know how important a college education is?

S: College is expensive. Besides, if I don't go to college now, I can start making money immediately. As soon as I earn **some,** I'd like to buy a car. Besides, my friends aren't going to college.

D: I'm not concerned about **them**. I'm interested in you and your future. I was just reading an article in a magazine about how much more money a college graduate earns than a high school graduate. Here's the article. Look at **it**. It says, "According to U.S. Census Bureau statistics, people with a bachelor's degree earn nearly twice as much as those with only a high school diploma. Over a lifetime, the gap in earning potential between a high school diploma and a B.A. (or higher) is more than $1,000,000."

S: Wow. I never realized that I could earn much more with a college degree than without **one**. But look here. The article also says, "In the 2008–2009 school year, the average tuition at a four-year private college was $25,143, and at a four-year public college, it was $6,585." How can you afford to send me to college?

D: I didn't just start to think about your college education today. I started to think about **it** when you were born. We saved money each month to buy a house, and we bought **one**. And we saved **some** each month for your college tuition.

S: That's great, Dad.

D: I also want you to apply for financial aid. There are grants, loans, and scholarships you should also look into. Your grades are good. I think you should apply for a scholarship.

S: I'll need to get an application.

D: I already thought of that. I brought **one** home today. Let's fill **it** out together.

S: Dad, if a college degree is so important to you, why didn't you get **one**?

D: When I was your age, we didn't live in the U.S. We were very poor and had to help our parents. You have a lot of opportunities for grants and scholarships, but we didn't have **any** when I was young.

S: Thanks for thinking about this from the day I was born.

Grants and Scholarships

Grants and scholarships provide aid that does not have to be repaid. However, **some** require that recipients maintain good grades or take certain courses.

Loans

Loans are another type of financial aid and are available to both students and parents. Like a car loan or a mortgage for a house, an education loan must eventually be repaid. Often, payments do not begin until the student finishes school. The interest rate on education loans is commonly lower than for other types of loans.

Amount You Would Need to Save to Have $10,000 Available When Your Child Begins College (Assuming a 5 percent interest rate.)					
			Amount Available When Child Begins College		
If you start saving when your child is	Number of years of saving	Approximate monthly savings	Principal	Interest earned	Total savings
Newborn	18	$29	$6,197	$3,803	$10,000
Age 4	14	41	6,935	3,065	10,000
Age 8	10	64	7,736	2,264	10,000
Age 12	6	119	8,601	1,399	10,000
Age 16	2	397	9,531	469	10,000

Source of chart: http://www.ed.gov/pubs/Prepare/pt4.html

14.9 Definite and Indefinite Pronouns

EXAMPLES	EXPLANATION
I've always thought about *your education*. I started to think about **it** when you were born. I received *two college applications*. I have to fill **them** out. The father wants *his son* to go to college. The father is going to help **him**.	We use definite pronouns *him, her, them,* and *it* to refer to definite count nouns.
A college degree is important. It's hard to make a lot of money without **one**. I don't have *a scholarship*. I hope I can get **one**.	We use the indefinite pronoun *one* to refer to an indefinite singular count noun.
a. The father knew it was important to save *money*. He saved **some** every month. b. I received *five brochures* for colleges. Did you receive **any**? c. You have a lot of *opportunities* today. When I was your age, we didn't have **any**.	We use *some* (for affirmative statements) and *any* (for negative statements and questions) to refer to an indefinite noncount noun (a) or an indefinite plural count noun (b) and (c).

Language Note: We often use *any* and *some* before *more*.
   Dad, I don't have enough money. I need **some more**.
   Son, I'm not going to give you **any more**.

EXERCISE 14 **A mother (M) is talking to her teenage daughter (D) about art school. Fill in the blanks with *one* or *it*.**

CD 4, TR 25

M: I have some information about the state university. Do you want to look at ____**it**____ with me?
(example)

D: I don't know, Mom. I don't know if I'm ready to go to college when I graduate.

M: Why not? We've been planning for _____ *(1)* since the day you were born.

D: College is not for everyone. I want to be an artist.

M: You can go to college and major in art. I checked out information about the art curriculum at the state university. It seems to have a very good program. Do you want to see information about _____? *(2)*

D: I'm not really interested in college. To be an artist, I don't need a college degree.

(continued)

M: But it's good to have _____ anyway.
(3)

D: I don't know why. In college, I'll have to study general courses, too, like

math and biology. You know I hate math. I'm not good at _____.
(4)

M: Well, maybe we should look at art schools. There's one downtown.

Do you want to visit _____?
(5)

D: Yes, I'd like to. We can probably find information about _____
(6)

on the Web too.

(*Looking at the art school's Web site*)

D: This school sounds great. Let's call and ask for an application.

M: I think you can get _____ online. Oh, yes, here it is.
(7)

D: Let's print a copy of _____.
(8)

M: You can fill _____ out online and submit _____
(9)   (10)

electronically.

EXERCISE 15   **ABOUT YOU**   Answer each question. Substitute the underlined words with an indefinite pronoun (*one, some, any*) or a definite pronoun (*it, them*).

EXAMPLES   Do you have <u>a pen</u> with you?
Yes, I have one.

Are you using <u>your pen</u> now?
No. I'm not using it now.

1. Does this school have <u>a library</u>?
2. How often do you use <u>the library</u>?
3. Do you have <u>a dictionary</u>?
4. When do you use <u>your dictionary</u>?
5. Did you buy <u>any textbooks</u> this semester?
6. How much did you pay for <u>your textbooks</u>?
7. Did the teacher give <u>any homework</u> last week?
8. Where did you do <u>the homework</u>?
9. Do you have any <u>American neighbors</u>?
10. Do you know <u>your neighbors</u>?
11. Does this school have <u>a cafeteria</u>?

12. Do you use <u>the cafeteria</u>?

13. Did you receive <u>any mail</u> today?

14. What time does your letter carrier deliver <u>your mail</u>?

EXERCISE 16 **This is a conversation between a teenage girl (A) and her mother (B). Fill in the blanks with *one, some, any, it, them, a, an, the,* or Ø (for no article).**

CD 4, TR 26

A: Can I have 15 dollars?

B: What for?

A: I have to buy ____*a*____ poster of my favorite singer.

(example)

B: I gave you _____ money last week. What did you do

(1)

with _____?

(2)

A: I spent _____ on a CD.

(3)

B: No, you can't have _____ more money until next

(4)

week. Besides, why do you need a poster? You already

have _____ in your room.

(5)

A: I took _____ down. I don't even like that singer anymore.

(6)

B: What happened to all _____ money Grandpa gave you for

(7)

your birthday?

A: I don't have _____ more money. I spent _____.

(8) (9)

B: You have to learn that _____ money doesn't grow on trees.

(10)

If you want me to give you _____, you'll have to work for it.

(11)

You can start by cleaning your room.

A: But I cleaned _____ two weeks ago.

(12)

B: That was two weeks ago. It's dirty again.

A: I don't have _____ time. I have to meet my friends.

(13)

B: You can't go out. You need to do your homework.

A: I don't have _____. Please let me have 15 dollars.

(14)

B: When I was your age, I had _____ job.

(15)

(continued)

Articles; *Other/Another*; Indefinite Pronouns **459**

A: I wanted to get a job last summer, but I couldn't find _____.
(16)

B: You didn't try hard enough. When I worked, I gave my parents

half of _____ money I earned. You kids today have
(17)

_____ easy life.
(18)

A: Why do _____ parents always say that to _____ kids?
(19)   (20)

B: Because it's true. It's time you learn that _____ life is hard.
(21)

A: I bet Grandpa said that to you when you were _____ child.
(22)

B: And I bet you'll say it to your kids when you're _____ adult.
(23)

Summary of Lesson 14

1. Articles

INDEFINITE

	Count—Singular	Count—Plural	Noncount
General	*A/An* **A child** likes toys.	Ø Article **Children** like toys. I love **children**.	Ø Article **Money** can't buy happiness. Everyone needs **money**.
Indefinite	*A/An* I bought **a toy**.	*Some/Any* I bought **some toys**. I didn't buy **any games**.	*Some/Any* I spent **some money**. I didn't buy **any candy**.
Classification	*A/An* A toddler is **a young child**.	Ø Article Teenagers are **young adults**.	_____

DEFINITE

	Count—Singular	Count—Plural	Noncount
Specific	**The toy** on the floor is for the baby. **The teacher** is explaining the grammar.	**The toys** on the table are for you. **The students** are listening to the teacher.	**The money** on the table is mine. **The information** about definite articles is helpful.
Unique	**The Internet** is a great tool.	**The Hawaiian Islands** are beautiful.	_____

2. Other/Another

	Definite	Indefinite
Singular	the other book my other book the other one the other	another book some/any other book my other book another one another
Plural	the other books my other books the other ones the others	other books some/any other books my other books other ones others

3. Indefinite Pronouns—Use *one/some/any* to substitute for indefinite nouns.
I need a quarter. Do you have **one**?
I need some pennies. You have **some**.
I don't have any change. Do you have **any**?

Editing Advice

1. Use *the* after a quantity word when the noun is definite.

      the
Most of students in my class are from Romania.

2. Be careful with *most* and *almost*.

      Most of
~~Almost~~ my teachers are very patient.

3. Use a plural count noun after a quantity expression.

      s
A few of my friend live in Canada.

4. *Another* is always singular.

      Other
Some teachers are strict. ~~Another~~ teachers are easy.

5. Use an indefinite pronoun to substitute for an indefinite noun.

      one
I need to borrow a pen. I didn't bring ~~it~~ today.

6. *A* and *an* are always singular.

She has ~~a~~ beautiful eyes.

7. Use *a* or *an* for a definition or a classification of a singular count noun.

                      a
The Statue of Liberty is ⌃ monument.

Editing Quiz

Some of the shaded words and phrases have mistakes. Find the mistakes and correct them. If the shaded words are correct, write *C*.

                C
I'm a teenager and I know this: ~~the~~ teenagers think about
   (example)   *(example)*

the money. They want money to buy a new jeans or sneakers. Or they
(1)   *(2)*   *(3)*

want money to go out with their friends. They might want to go to the
                                                            (4)

restaurant or to a movie. Almost my friends try to get a job in the summer
             (5)   *(6)*

to make some money. At the beginning of every summer, my friends always
        (7)

say, "I need a job. Do you know where I can find it?"
             (8)   *(9)*

One of my friend found a summer job at Bender's. Bender's is
              (10)

big bookstore. Another friend found a job at a summer camp. But I have
(11)   *(12)*

the other way to make money. I prefer to work in my neighborhood.
(13)

Most of people in my neighborhood are working or elderly. I ask my
    (14)

neighbors if they have a work for me. Some neighbors pay me to take care
                  (15)

of the lawn in front of their house. Another neighbors pay me to clean
  (16)   *(17)*

their garage. In the winter, I shovel sidewalks in front of their houses. I like
                                (18)

these jobs. I love a music and I listen to my favorite music while I work.
               (19)

What do I do with the money I get from my jobs? I buy songs on
                    (20)

Internet. I used to buy CDs, but I only liked a few songs. Some of songs
(21)   *(22)*

on the CDs were great but I never listened to anothers. Now I can download
                                    (23)

the songs I like and not pay for all the other songs on a CD. This helps me
(24)   *(25)*

save money. I have an old MP3 player I got from my grandfather for my

twelfth birthday, but I want to buy other one. The new ones are smaller
                           (26)   *(27)*

and hold more songs. If I keep working hard, I know I'll be able to buy all the
                                                                       (28)

things I want.

Lesson 14 Test/Review

PART 1 Fill in the blanks with *the, a, an, some, any,* or *Ø* (for no article). In some cases, more than one answer is possible.

A: Do you want to come to my house tonight? I rented _____*some*_____
(example)

movies. We can make _____ popcorn and watch
(1)

_____ movies together.
(2)

B: Thanks, but I'm going to _____ party. Do you want to
(3)

go with me?

A: Where's it going to be?

B: It's going to be at Michael's apartment.

A: Who's going to be at _____ party?
(4)

B: Most of _____ students in my English class will be there. Each
(5)

student is going to bring _____ food.
(6)

A: In the U.S. _____ life is strange. In my country, _____
(7)   (8)

people don't have to bring _____ food to a party.
(9)

B: That's the way it is in my country, too. But we're in _____
(10)

U.S. now. I'm going to bake _____ cake. You can make
(11)

_____ special dish from your country.
(12)

A: You know I'm _____ terrible cook.
(13)

B: Don't worry. You can buy something. My friend Max is going

to buy _____ crackers and cheese. Why don't you bring
(14)

_____ salami or roast beef?
(15)

A: But I don't eat _____ meat. I'm _____ vegetarian.
(16)   (17)

B: Well, you can bring _____ bowl of fruit.
(18)

A: That's _____ good idea. What time does _____
(19)   (20)

party start?

B: At 8 P.M.

(continued)

A: I have to take my brother to _____ airport at 6:30. I don't know
(21)
if I'll be back on time.

B: You don't have to arrive at 8:00 exactly. I'll give you _____
(22)
address, and you can arrive any time you want.

PART **2** **Fill in the blanks with *other, others, another,* or *the other*.**

A: I don't like my apartment.

B: Why not?

A: It's very small. It only has two closets. One is big, but ____the other____
(example)
is very small.

B: That's not very serious. Is that the only problem? Are there

_____ problems?
(1)

A: There are many _____.
(2)

B: Such as?

A: Well, the landlord doesn't provide enough heat in the winter.

B: Hmm. That's a real problem. Did you complain to him?

A: I did, but he says that all _____ tenants are happy.
(3)

B: Why don't you look for _____ apartment?
(4)

A: I have two roommates. One wants to move, but _____
(5)
likes it here.

B: Well, if one wants to stay and _____ two want to move,
(6)
why don't you move and look for _____ roommate?
(7)

PART **3** **Fill in the blanks with *one, some, any, it,* or *them*.**

EXAMPLE I have a computer, but my roommate doesn't have ____one____.

1. Do you want to use my bicycle? I won't need _____ this
afternoon.

2. I rented a movie. We can watch _____ tonight.

3. My English teacher gives some homework every day, but she doesn't
give _____ on the weekends.

4. My class has a lot of Mexican students. Does your class have

    _____?

5. I wrote two compositions last week, but I got bad grades because
   I wrote _____ very quickly.

6. I don't have any problems with English, but my roommate
   has _____.

7. I can't remember the teacher's name. Do you remember _____?

8. You won't need any paper for the test, but you'll need _____ for
   the composition.

9. I went to the library to find some books in my language, but I couldn't
   find _____.

Expansion

Classroom
Activities

Fill in the blanks with *all*, *most*, *some*, *a few*, or *very few* to make a general statement about your native country or another country you know well. Find a partner from a different country, if possible, and compare your answers.

a. _____ banks are safe places to put your money.

b. _____ doctors make a lot of money.

c. _____ teenagers work.

d. _____ children work.

e. _____ teachers are rich.

f. _____ government officials are rich.

g. _____ children get an allowance.

h. _____ people work on Saturdays.

i. _____ businesses are closed on Sundays.

j. _____ families own a car.

k. _____ women work outside the home.

l. _____ people have a college education.

m. _____ people have servants.

n. _____ married couples have their own apartment.

o. _____ old people live with their grown children.

p. _____ people speak English.

q. _____ children study English in school.

Talk

About It **❶** The following sayings and proverbs are about money. Discuss the meaning of each one. Do you have a similar saying in your native language?

- All that glitters isn't gold.
- Money is the root of all evil.
- Friendship and money don't mix.
- Another day, another dollar.
- Money talks.

❷ Discuss ways to save money. Discuss difficulties in saving money.

❸ Discuss this saying: The difference between men and boys is the price of their toys.

Write

About It **❶** Do you think kids should get an allowance from their parents? How much? Does it depend on the child's age? Should the child have to work for the money? Write a few paragraphs explaining your point of view.

❷ Write a short composition giving advice to teenagers on how to earn and save money.

How Teenagers Can Make Money

Teenagers often want to make some money. One way to make money is by taking a job in the summer. Teenagers can work at fast-food restaurants or summer camps, or by doing gardening work for their neighbors. Another way to make money . . .

 For more practice using grammar in context, please visit our Web site.

Appendices

Appendix A

Spelling and Pronunciation of Verbs

Spelling of the -s Form of Verbs

Rule	Base Form	-s Form
Add -s to most verbs to make the -s form.	hope eat	hopes eats
When the base form ends in *ss*, *zz*, *sh*, *ch*, or *x*, add -es and pronounce an extra syllable, /əz/.	miss buzz wash catch fix	misses buzzes washes catches fixes
When the base form ends in a consonant + *y*, change the *y* to *i* and add -es.	carry worry	carries worries
When the base form ends in a vowel + *y*, do not change the *y*.	pay obey	pays obeys
Add -es to *go* and *do*.	go do	goes does

Three Pronunciations of the -s Form			
We pronounce /**s**/ if the verb ends in these voiceless sounds: /**p t k f**/.	hope—hopes eat—eats	pick—picks laugh—laughs	
We pronounce /**z**/ if the verb ends in most voiced sounds.	live—lives grab—grabs read—reads	run—runs sing—sings borrow—borrows	
When the base form ends in *ss*, *zz*, *sh*, *ch*, *x*, *se*, *ge*, or *ce*, we pronounce an extra syllable, /**əz**/.	miss—misses buzz—buzzes wash—washes watch—watches	fix—fixes use—uses change—changes dance—dances	
These verbs have a change in the vowel sound.	do/**du**/—does/**dəz**/	say/**sei**/—says/**sez**/	

Spelling of the *-ing* Form of Verbs

Rule	Base Form	*-ing* Form
Add *-ing* to most verbs. **Note:** Do not remove the *y* for the *-ing* form.	eat go study carry	eating going studying carrying
For a one-syllable verb that ends in a consonant + vowel + consonant (CVC), double the final consonant and add *-ing*.	p l a n 　C V C s t o p 　C V C s i t C V C g r a b 　C V C	planning stopping sitting grabbing
Do not double the final *w*, *x*, or *y*.	show mix stay	showing mixing staying
For a two-syllable word that ends in CVC, double the final consonant only if the last syllable is stressed.	refér admít begín rebél	referring admitting beginning rebelling
When the last syllable of a multi-syllable word is not stressed, do not double the final consonant.	lísten ópen óffer límit devélop	listening opening offering limiting developing
If the word ends in a consonant + *e*, drop the *e* before adding *-ing*.	live take write arrive	living taking writing arriving

Spelling of the Past Tense of Regular Verbs

Rule	Base Form	-ed Form
Add -ed to the base form to make the past tense of most regular verbs.	start kick	started kicked
When the base form ends in e, add -d only.	die live	died lived
When the base form ends in a consonant + y, change the y to i and add -ed.	carry worry	carried worried
When the base form ends in a vowel + y, do not change the y.	destroy stay	destroyed stayed
For a one-syllable word that ends in a consonant + vowel + consonant (CVC), double the final consonant and add -ed.	s t o p | | | C V C p l u g | | | C V C	stopped plugged
Do not double the final w or x.	sew fix	sewed fixed
For a two-syllable word that ends in CVC, double the final consonant only if the last syllable is stressed.	occúr permít	occurred permitted
When the last syllable of a multi-syllable word is not stressed, do not double the final consonant.	ópen háppen devélop	opened happened developed

Pronunciation of Past Forms that End in -ed

The past tense with -ed has three pronunciations.			
We pronounce a /**t**/ if the base form ends in these voiceless sounds: /**p, k, f, s, š, č**/.	jump—jumped cook—cooked	cough—coughed kiss—kissed	wash—washed watch—watched
We pronounce a /**d**/ if the base form ends in most voiced sounds.	rub—rubbed drag—dragged love—loved bathe—bathed use—used	charge—charged glue—glued massage—massaged name—named learn—learned	bang—banged call—called fear—feared free—freed stay—stayed
We pronounce an extra syllable /**ə d**/ if the base form ends in a /**t**/ or /**d**/ sound.	wait—waited hate—hated	want—wanted add—added	need—needed decide—decided

Appendix B

Irregular Noun Plurals

Singular	Plural	Explanation
man woman tooth foot goose	men women teeth feet geese	Vowel change (**Note:** The first vowel in *women* is pronounced /I/.)
sheep fish deer	sheep fish deer	No change
child person mouse	children people (OR persons) mice	Different word form
	(eye)glasses belongings clothes goods groceries jeans pajamas pants/slacks scissors shorts	No singular form
alumnus cactus radius stimulus syllabus	alumni cacti (OR cactuses) radii stimuli syllabi (OR syllabuses)	*us → i*
analysis crisis hypothesis oasis parenthesis thesis	analyses crises hypotheses oases parentheses theses	*is → es*
appendix index	appendices (OR appendixes) indices (OR indexes)	*ix → ices* OR *→ ixes* *ex → ices* OR *→ exes*

Singular	Plural	Explanation
bacterium	bacteria	$um \rightarrow a$
curriculum	curricula	
datum	data	
medium	media	
memorandum	memoranda	
criterion	criteria	$ion \rightarrow a$
phenomenon	phenomena	$on \rightarrow a$
alga	algae	$a \rightarrow ae$
formula	formulae (OR formulas)	
vertebra	vertebrae	

Appendix C

Spelling Rules for Adverbs Ending in -ly

Adjective Ending	Examples	Adverb Ending	Adverb
Most endings	careful quiet serious	Add -ly.	carefully quietly seriously
y	easy happy lucky	Change y to i and add -ly.	easily happily luckily
e	nice free	Keep the e and add -ly.*	nicely freely
consonant + le	simple comfortable double	Drop the e and add -ly.	simply comfortably doubly
ic	basic enthusiastic	Add -ally.**	basically enthusiastically
Exceptions: 　*true—truly 　**public—publicly			

Appendix D

Metric Conversion Chart

Length

When You Know	Symbol	Multiply by	To Find	Symbol
inches	in	2.54	centimeters	cm
feet	ft	30.5	centimeters	cm
feet	ft	0.3	meters	m
yards	yd	0.91	meters	m
miles	mi	1.6	kilometers	km
Metric:				
centimeters	cm	0.39	inches	in
centimeters	cm	0.03	feet	ft
meters	m	3.28	feet	ft
meters	m	1.09	yards	yd
kilometers	km	0.62	miles	mi

Note:
12 inches = 1 foot
3 feet / 36 inches = 1 yard

Area

When You Know	Symbol	Multiply by	To Find	Symbol
square inches	in²	6.5	square centimeters	cm²
square feet	ft²	0.09	square meters	m²
square yards	yd²	0.8	square meters	m²
square miles	mi²	2.6	square kilometers	km²
Metric:				
square centimeters	cm²	0.16	square inches	in²
square meters	m²	10.76	square feet	ft²
square meters	m²	1.2	square yards	yd²
square kilometers	km²	0.39	square miles	mi²

Weight (Mass)

When You Know	Symbol	Multiply by	To Find	Symbol
ounces	oz	28.35	grams	g
pounds	lb	0.45	kilograms	kg
Metric:				
grams	g	0.04	ounces	oz
kilograms	kg	2.2	pounds	lb
Note: 1 pound = 16 ounces				

Volume

When You Know	Symbol	Multiply by	To Find	Symbol
fluid ounces	fl oz	30.0	milliliters	mL
pints	pt	0.47	liters	L
quarts	qt	0.95	liters	L
gallons	gal	3.8	liters	L
Metric:				
milliliters	mL	0.03	fluid ounces	fl oz
liters	L	2.11	pints	pt
liters	L	1.05	quarts	qt
liters	L	0.26	gallons	gal

Temperature

When You Know	Symbol	Do this	To Find	Symbol
degrees Fahrenheit	°F	Subtract 32, then multiply by $5/9$	degrees Celsius	°C
Metric:				
degrees Celsius	°C	Multiply by $9/5$, then add 32	degrees Fahrenheit	°F

Sample temperatures

Fahrenheit	Celsius
0	– 18
10	–12
20	–7
32	0
40	4
50	10
60	16
70	21
80	27
90	32
100	38
212	100

Appendix E

The Verb *GET*

Get has many meanings. Here is a list of the most common ones:

- get something = receive
  I got a letter from my father.

- get + (to) place = arrive
  I got home at six. What time do you get to school?

- get + object + infinitive = persuade
  She got him to wash the dishes.

- get + past participle = become

get acquainted	get worried	get hurt	get engaged
get lost	get bored	get married	get accustomed to
get confused	get divorced	get used to	get scared
get tired	get dressed		

  They got married in 1989.

- get + adjective = become

get hungry	get sleepy	get rich	get dark	get nervous
get angry	get well	get old	get upset	get fat

  It gets dark at 6:30.

- get an illness = catch
  While she was traveling, she got malaria.

- get a joke or an idea = understand
  Everybody except Tom laughed at the joke. He didn't get it.
  The boss explained the project to us, but I didn't get it.

- get ahead = advance
  He works very hard because he wants to get ahead in his job.

- get along (well) (with someone) = have a good relationship
  She doesn't get along with her mother-in-law.
  Do you and your roommate get along well?

- get around to something = find the time to do something
  I wanted to write my brother a letter yesterday, but I didn't get around to it.

- get away = escape
  The police chased the thief, but he got away.

- get away with something = escape punishment
  He cheated on his taxes and got away with it.

- get back = return
  He got back from his vacation last Saturday.

- get back at someone = get revenge
  My brother wants to get back at me for stealing his girlfriend.

- get back to someone = communicate with someone at a later time
  The boss can't talk to you today. Can she get back to you tomorrow?

- get by = have just enough but nothing more
  On her salary, she's just getting by. She can't afford a car or a vacation.

- get in trouble = be caught and punished for doing something wrong
  They got in trouble for cheating on the test.

- get in(to) = enter a car
  She got in the car and drove away quickly.

- get out (of) = leave a car
  When the taxi arrived at the theater, everyone got out.

- get on = seat yourself on a bicycle, motorcycle, horse
  She got on the motorcycle and left.

- get on = enter a train, bus, airplane
  She got on the bus and took a seat in the back.

- get off = leave a bicycle, motorcycle, horse, train, bus, airplane
  They will get off the train at the next stop.

- get out of something = escape responsibility
  My boss wants me to help him on Saturday, but I'm going to try to get out of it.

(continued)

- get over something = recover from an illness or disappointment
  She has the flu this week. I hope she gets over it soon.

- get rid of someone or something = free oneself of someone or something undesirable
  My apartment has roaches, and I can't get rid of them.

- get through (to someone) = communicate, often by telephone
  I tried to call my mother many times, but her line was busy. I couldn't get through.

- get through (with something) = finish
  I can meet you after I get through with my homework.

- get together = meet with another person
  I'd like to see you again. When can we get together?

- get up = arise from bed
  He woke up at six o'clock, but he didn't get up until 6:30.

Appendix F

MAKE and DO

Some expressions use make. Others use do.

Make	Do
make a date/an appointment	do (the) homework
make a plan	do an exercise
make a decision	do the cleaning, laundry, dishes, washing, etc.
make a telephone call	do the shopping
make a meal (breakfast, lunch, dinner)	do one's best
make a mistake	do a favor
make an effort	do the right/wrong thing
make an improvement	do a job
make a promise	do business
make money	What do you do for a living? (asks about a job)
make noise	How do you do? (said when you
make the bed	meet someone for the first time)

Appendix G

Prepositions of Time

- **in** the morning: He takes a shower *in* the morning.
- **in** the afternoon: He takes a shower *in* the afternoon.
- **in** the evening: He takes a shower *in* the evening.
- **at** night: He takes a shower *at* night.
- **in** the summer, fall, winter, spring: He takes classes *in* the summer.
- **on** that/this day: May 4 is my birthday. I became a citizen *on* that day.
- **on** the weekend: He studies *on* the weekend.
- **on** a specific day: His birthday is *on* March 5.
- **in** a month: His birthday is *in* March.
- **in** a year: He was born *in* 1978.
- **in** a century: People didn't use cars *in* the 19th century.
- **on** a day: I don't have class *on* Monday.
- **at** a specific time: My class begins *at* 12:30.
- **from** a time **to** (OR **till** OR **until**) another time: My class is *from* 12:30 *to* (OR *till* OR *until*) 3:30.
- **in** a number of hours, days, weeks, months, years: She will graduate *in* three weeks. (This means "after" three weeks.)
- **for** a number of hours, days, weeks, months, years: She was in Mexico *for* three weeks. (This means during the period of three weeks.)
- **by** a time: Please finish your test *by* six o'clock. (This means "no later than" six o'clock.)
- **until** a time: I lived with my parents *until* I came to the U.S. (This means "all the time before.")
- **during** the movie, class, meeting: He slept *during* the meeting.
- **about/around** six o'clock: The movie will begin *about* six o'clock. People will arrive *around* 5:45.
- **in** the past/future: *In* the past, she never exercised.
- **at** present: *At* present, the days are getting longer.
- **in** the beginning/end: *In* the beginning, she didn't understand the teacher at all.
- **at** the beginning/end of something: The semester begins *at* the beginning of September. My birthday is *at* the end of June.
- **before/after** a time: You should finish the job *before* Friday. The library will be closed *after* six o'clock.
- **before/after** an action takes place: Turn off the lights *before* you leave. Wash the dishes *after* you finish dinner.

Verbs and Adjectives Followed by a Preposition

Many verbs and adjectives are followed by a preposition.

accuse someone of
(be) accustomed to
adjust to
(be) afraid of
agree with
(be) amazed at/by
(be) angry about
(be) angry at/with
apologize for
approve of
argue about
argue with
(be) ashamed of
(be) aware of
believe in
blame someone for
(be) bored with/by
(be) capable of
care about
care for
compare to/with
complain about
(be) concerned about
concentrate on
consist of
count on
deal with
decide on
depend on/upon
(be) different from
disapprove of
(be) divorced from
dream about/of
(be) engaged to
(be) excited about

(be) familiar with
(be) famous for
feel like
(be) fond of
forget about
forgive someone for
(be) glad about
(be) good at
(be) grateful to someone for
(be) guilty of
(be) happy about
hear about
hear of
hope for
(be) incapable of
insist on/upon
(be) interested in
(be) involved in
(be) jealous of
(be) known for
(be) lazy about
listen to
look at
look for
look forward to
(be) mad about
(be) mad at
(be) made from/of
(be) married to
object to
(be) opposed to
participate in
plan on
pray to
pray for

(be) prepared for/to
prevent (someone) from
prohibit (someone) from
protect (someone) from
(be) proud of
recover from
(be) related to
rely on/upon
(be) responsible for
(be) sad about
(be) satisfied with
(be) scared of
(be) sick of
(be) sorry about
(be) sorry for
speak about
speak to/with
succeed in
(be) sure of/about
(be) surprised at
take care of
talk about
talk to/with
thank (someone) for
(be) thankful (to someone) for
think about/of
(be) tired of
(be) upset about
(be) upset with
(be) used to
wait for
warn (someone) about
(be) worried about
worry about

Appendix I

Direct and Indirect Objects

> The order of direct and indirect objects depends on the verb you use. It also can depend on whether you use a noun or a pronoun as the object.

Group 1 Pronouns affect word order. The preposition used is *to*.

Patterns:
He gave a present to his wife. (DO to IO)
He gave his wife a present. (IO/DO)
He gave it to his wife. (DO to IO)
He gave her a present. (IO/DO)
He gave it to her. (DO to IO)

Verbs:

bring	lend	pass	sell	show	teach
give	offer	pay	send	sing	tell
hand	owe	read	serve	take	write

Group 2 Pronouns affect word order. The preposition used is *for*.

Patterns:
He bought a car for his daughter. (DO for IO)
He bought his daughter a car. (IO/DO)
He bought it for his daughter. (DO for IO)
He bought her a car. (IO/DO)
He bought it for her. (DO for IO)

Verbs:

bake	buy	draw	get	make
build	do	find	knit	reserve

Group 3 Pronouns don't affect word order. The preposition used is *to*.

Patterns:
He explained the problem to his friend. (DO to IO)
He explained it to her. (DO to IO)

Verbs:

admit	introduce	recommend	say
announce	mention	repeat	speak
describe	prove	report	suggest
explain			

Group 4 Pronouns don't affect word order. The preposition used is *for*.

Patterns:
He cashed a check for his friend. (DO for IO)
He cashed it for her. (DO for IO)

Verbs:

answer	change	design	open	prescribe
cash	close	fix	prepare	pronounce

Group 5 Pronouns don't affect word order. No preposition is used.

Patterns:
She asked the teacher a question. (IO/DO)
She asked him a question. (IO/DO)

Verbs:

ask	charge	cost	wish	take (with time)

Capitalization Rules

- The first word in a sentence: **My** friends are helpful.

- The word "I": My sister and **I** took a trip together.

- Names of people: **J**ulia **R**oberts; **G**eorge **W**ashington

- Titles preceding names of people: **D**octor (**D**r.) **S**mith; **P**resident **L**incoln; **Q**ueen **E**lizabeth; **M**r. **R**ogers; **M**rs. **C**arter

- Geographic names: the **U**nited **S**tates; **L**ake **S**uperior; **C**alifornia; the **R**ocky **M**ountains; the **M**ississippi **R**iver

    NOTE: The word "the" in a geographic name is not capitalized.

- Street names: **P**ennsylvania **A**venue (**A**ve.); **W**all **S**treet (**S**t.); **A**bbey **R**oad (**R**d.)

- Names of organizations, companies, colleges, buildings, stores, hotels: the **R**epublican **P**arty; **H**einle **C**engage; **D**artmouth **C**ollege; the **U**niversity of **W**isconsin; the **W**hite **H**ouse; **B**loomingdale's; the **H**ilton **H**otel

- Nationalities and ethnic groups: **M**exicans; **C**anadians; **S**paniards; **A**mericans; **J**ews; **K**urds; **E**skimos

- Languages: **E**nglish; **S**panish; **P**olish; **V**ietnamese; **R**ussian

- Months: **J**anuary; **F**ebruary

- Days: **S**unday; **M**onday

- Holidays: **C**hristmas; **I**ndependence **D**ay

- Important words in a title: *Grammar in Context*; *The Old Man and the Sea*; *Romeo and Juliet*; *The Sound of Music*

    NOTE: Capitalize "the" as the first word of a title.

Glossary of Grammatical Terms

- **Adjective** An adjective gives a description of a noun.

  It's a *tall* tree.   He's an *old* man.   My neighbors are *nice*.

- **Adverb** An adverb describes the action of a sentence or an adjective or another adverb.

  She speaks English *fluently*.   I drive *carefully*.
  She speaks English *extremely* well.   She is *very* intelligent.

- **Adverb of Frequency** An adverb of frequency tells how often the action happens.

  I *never* drink coffee.   They *usually* take the bus.

- **Affirmative** means *yes*.

- **Apostrophe '** We use the apostrophe for possession and contractions.

  My *sister's* friend is beautiful.   Today *isn't* Sunday.

- **Article** The definite article is *the*. The indefinite articles are *a* and *an*.

  I have *a* cat.   I ate *an* apple.   *The* teacher came late.

- **Auxiliary Verb** Some verbs have two parts: an auxiliary verb and a main verb.

  He *can't* study.   We *will* return.

- **Base Form** The base form, sometimes called the "simple" form, of the verb has no tense. It has no ending (*-s* or *-ed*): *be, go, eat, take, write*.

  I didn't *go* out.   We don't *know* you.   He can't *drive*.

- **Capital Letter** A B C D E F G . . .

- **Clause** A clause is a group of words that has a subject and a verb. Some sentences have only one clause.

  She speaks Spanish.

Some sentences have **a main clause** and a **dependent clause**.

MAIN CLAUSE	DEPENDENT CLAUSE (**reason clause**)
She found a good job	because she has computer skills.

MAIN CLAUSE	DEPENDENT CLAUSE (**time clause**)
She'll turn off the light	before she goes to bed.

MAIN CLAUSE	DEPENDENT CLAUSE (**if clause**)
I'll take you to the doctor	if you don't have your car on Saturday.

(continued)

- **Colon** :
- **Comma** ,
- **Comparative Form** A comparative form of an adjective or adverb is used to compare two things.

  > My house is *bigger* than your house.
  > Her husband drives *faster* than she does.

- **Complement** The complement of the sentence is the information after the verb. It completes the verb phrase.

  > He works *hard.*   I slept *for five hours.*   They are *late.*

- **Consonant** The following letters are consonants: *b, c, d, f, g, h, j, k, l, m, n, p, q, r, s, t, v, w, x, y, z.*

  > NOTE: *y* is sometimes considered a vowel, as in the world *syllable.*

- **Contraction** A contraction is made up of two words put together with an apostrophe.

  > *He's* my brother.   *You're* late.   They *won't* talk to me.
  > (*He's* = he is)   (*You're* = you are)   (*won't* = will not*)

- **Count Noun** Count nouns are nouns that we can count. They have a singular and a plural form.

  > 1 pen — 3 pens   1 table — 4 tables

- **Dependent Clause** See **Clause.**
- **Direct Object** A direct object is a noun (phrase) or pronoun that receives the action of the verb.

  > We saw *the movie.*   You have *a nice car.*   I love *you.*

- **Exclamation Mark** !
- **Frequency Words** Frequency words are *always, usually, generally, often, sometimes, rarely, seldom, hardly ever, never.*

  > I *never* drink coffee.   We *always* do our homework.

- **Hyphen** –
- **Imperative** An imperative sentence gives a command or instructions. An imperative sentence omits the word *you.*

  > *Come* here.   *Don't be* late.   Please *sit* down.

- **Infinitive** An infinitive is *to* + base form.

  > I want *to leave.*   You need *to be* here on time.

- **Linking Verb** A linking verb is a verb that links the subject to the noun or adjective after it. Linking verbs include *be, seem, feel, smell, sound, look, appear, taste.*

  > She *is* a doctor.   She *seems* very intelligent.   She *looks* tired.

- **Modal** The modal verbs are *can, could, shall, should, will, would, may, might, must.*

  They *should* leave.   I *must* go.

- **Negative** means no.

- **Nonaction Verb** A nonaction verb has no action. We do not use a continuous tense (*be* + verb *-ing*) with a nonaction verb. The nonaction verbs are: *believe, cost, care, have, hear, know, like, love, matter, mean, need, own, prefer, remember, see, seem, think, understand, want,* and sense-perception verbs.

  She *has* a laptop.   We *love* our mother.   You *look* great.

- **Noncount Noun** A noncount noun is a noun that we don't count. It has no plural form.

  She drank some *water.*   He prepared some *rice.*
  Do you need any *money?*   We had a lot of *homework.*

- **Noun** A noun is a person (*brother*), a place (*kitchen*), or a thing (*table*). Nouns can be either count (*1 table, 2 tables*) or noncount (*money, water*).

  My *brother* lives in California.   My *sisters* live in New York.
  I get *advice* from them.   I drink *coffee* every day.

- **Noun Modifier** A noun modifier makes a noun more specific.

  fire department   *Independence* Day   *can* opener

- **Noun Phrase** A noun phrase is a group of words that form the subject or object of the sentence.

  A *very nice woman* helped me at registration.
  I bought *a big box of cereal.*

- **Object** The object of the sentence follows the verb. It receives the action of the verb.

  He bought *a car.*   I saw *a movie.*   I met *your brother.*

- **Object Pronoun** Use object pronouns (*me, you, him, her, it, us, them*) after the verb or preposition.

  He likes *her.*   I saw the movie. Let's talk about *it.*

- **Parentheses** ( )

- **Paragraph** A paragraph is a group of sentences about one topic.

- **Participle, Present** The present participle is verb + *-ing.*

  She is *sleeping.*   They were *laughing.*

- **Period** .

- **Phrase** A group of words that go together.

  Last month my sister came to visit.
  There is a strange car *in front of my house.*

(continued)

- **Plural** Plural means more than one. A plural noun usually ends with *-s*.

  She has beautiful *eyes*.   My *feet* are big.

- **Possessive Form** Possessive forms show ownership or relationship.

  Mary's coat is in the closet.   My *brother* lives in Miami.

- **Preposition** A preposition is a short connecting word: *about, above, across, after, around, as, at, away, back, before, behind, below, by, down, for, from, in, into, like, of, off, on, out, over, to, under, up, with.*

  The book is *on* the table.   She studies *with* her friends.

- **Pronoun** A pronoun takes the place of a noun.

  I have a new car. I bought *it* last week.
  John likes Mary, but *she* doesn't like *him*.

- **Punctuation** Period . Comma , Colon : Semicolon ; Question Mark ? Exclamation Mark !

- **Question Mark** ?

- **Quotation Marks** " "

- **Regular Verb** A regular verb forms its past tense with *-ed*.

  He *worked* yesterday.   I *laughed* at the joke.

- **-s Form** A present tense verb that ends in *-s* or *-es*.

  He *lives* in New York.   She *watches* TV a lot.

- **Sense-Perception Verb** A sense-perception verb has no action. It describes a sense. The sense perception verbs are: *look, feel, taste, sound, smell.*

  She *feels* fine.   The coffee *smells* fresh.   The milk *tastes* sour.

- **Sentence** A sentence is a group of words that contains a subject[1] and a verb (at least) and gives a complete thought.

  SENTENCE: She came home.
  NOT A SENTENCE: When she came home

- **Simple Form of Verb** The simple form of the verb, also called the base form, has no tense; it never has an *-s, -ed,* or *-ing* ending.

  Did you *see* the movie?   I couldn't *find* your phone number.

- **Singular** Singular means one.

  She ate a *sandwich*.   I have one *television*.

- **Subject** The subject of the sentence tells who or what the sentence is about.

  My *sister* got married last April. *The wedding* was beautiful.

[1]In an imperative sentence, the subject *you* is omitted: *Sit down. Come here.*

- **Subject Pronouns** Use subject pronouns (*I, you, he, she, it, we, you, they*) before a verb.

  They speak Japanese.   *We* speak Spanish.

- **Superlative Form** A superlative form of an adjective or adverb shows the number one item in a group of three or more.

  January is the *coldest* month of the year.
  My brother speaks English the *best* in my family.

- **Syllable** A syllable is a part of a word that has only one vowel sound. (Some words have only one syllable.)

  change (one syllable)   after (af·ter = two syllables)
  look (one syllable)   responsible (re·spon·si·ble = four syllables)

- **Tag Question** A tag question is a short question at the end of a sentence. It is used in conversation.

  You speak Spanish, *don't you?*   He's not happy, *is he?*

- **Tense** A verb has tense. Tense shows when the action of the sentence happened.

  SIMPLE PRESENT: She usually *works* hard.
  FUTURE: She *will work* tomorrow.
  PRESENT CONTINUOUS: She *is working* now.
  SIMPLE PAST: She *worked* yesterday.

- **Verb** A verb is the action of the sentence.

  He *runs* fast.   I *speak* English.

  Some verbs have no action. They are linking verbs. They connect the subject to the rest of the sentence.

  He *is* tall.   She *looks* beautiful.   You *seem* tired.

- **Vowel** The following letters are vowels: *a, e, i, o, u.* Y is sometimes considered a vowel (for example, in the word *mystery*).

Special Uses of Articles

No Article	Article

Personal names:
   John Kennedy
   Michael Jordan
	The whole family:
	   the Kennedys
	   the Jordans

Title and name:
   Queen Elizabeth
   Pope Benedict
	Title without name:
	   the Queen
	   the Pope

Cities, states, countries, continents:
   Cleveland
   Ohio
   Mexico
   South America
	Places that are considered a union:
	   the United States
	   the former Soviet Union
	   the United Kingdom
	Place names: the _____ of _____
	   the Republic of China
	   the District of Columbia

Mountains:
   Mount Everest
   Mount McKinley
	Mountain ranges:
	   the Himalayas
	   the Rocky Mountains

Islands:
   Coney Island
   Staten Island
	Collectives of islands:
	   the Hawaiian Islands
	   the Virgin Islands
	   the Philippines

Lakes:
   Lake Superior
   Lake Michigan
	Collectives of lakes:
	   the Great Lakes
	   the Finger Lakes

Beaches:
   Palm Beach
   Pebble Beach
	Rivers, oceans, seas, canals:
	   the Mississippi River
	   the Atlantic Ocean
	   the Dead Sea
	   the Panama Canal

Streets and avenues:
   Madison Avenue
   Wall Street
	Well-known buildings:
	   the Willis Tower
	   the Empire State Building

Parks:
   Central Park
   Hyde Park
	Zoos:
	   the San Diego Zoo
	   the Milwaukee Zoo

No Article	Article

Seasons:
    summer   fall
    spring   winter
    Summer is my favorite season.
NOTE: After a preposition, *the* may be used.
    In (the) winter, my car runs badly.
	Deserts:
	    the Mojave Desert
	    the Sahara Desert

Directions:
    north   south
    east   west
	Sections of a piece of land:
	    the Southwest (of the U.S.)
	    the West Side (of New York)

School subjects:
    history
    math
	Unique geographical points:
	    the North Pole
	    the Vatican

Name + *college* or *university*:
    Northwestern University
    Bradford College
	The University/College of _____:
	    the University of Michigan
	    the College of DuPage County

Magazines:
    Time
    Sports Illustrated
	Newspapers:
	    the *Tribune*
	    the *Wall Street Journal*

Months and days:
    September
    Monday
	Ships:
	    the *Titanic*
	    the *Queen Elizabeth*

Holidays and dates
    Thanksgiving
    Mother's Day
    July 4 (month + day)
	The day of the month:
	    the Fourth of July
	    the fifth of May

Diseases:
    cancer   AIDS
    polio   malaria
	Ailments:
	    a cold a toothache
	    a headache the flu

Games and sports:
    poker
    soccer
	Musical instruments, after *play*:
	    the drums
	    the piano
	NOTE: Sometimes *the* is omitted.
	    She plays (the) drums.

Languages:
    French
    English
	The _____ language:
	    the French language
	    the English language

Last month, year, week, etc. = the one before this one:
    I forgot to pay my rent last month.
    The teacher gave us a test last week.
	The last month, the last year, the last week, etc. = the last in a series:
	    December is the last month of the year.
	    Summer vacation begins the last week in May.

(continued)

No Article	Article

In office = in an elected position:
  The president is in office for four years.
	In the office = in a specific room:
	  The teacher is in the office.

In back/front:
  She's in back of
  the car.
	In the back/the front:
	  He's in the back of the bus.

Appendix M

Alphabetical List of Irregular Verb Forms

Base Form	Past Form	Past Participle	Base Form	Past Form	Past Participle
be	was/were	been	drink	drank	drunk
bear	bore	born/borne	drive	drove	driven
beat	beat	beaten	eat	ate	eaten
become	became	become	fall	fell	fallen
begin	began	begun	feed	fed	fed
bend	bent	bent	feel	felt	felt
bet	bet	bet	fight	fought	fought
bid	bid	bid	find	found	found
bind	bound	bound	fit	fit	fit
bite	bit	bitten	flee	fled	fled
bleed	bled	bled	fly	flew	flown
blow	blew	blown	forbid	forbade	forbidden
break	broke	broken	forget	forgot	forgotten
breed	bred	bred	forgive	forgave	forgiven
bring	brought	brought	freeze	froze	frozen
broadcast	broadcast	broadcast	get	got	gotten
build	built	built	give	gave	given
burst	burst	burst	go	went	gone
buy	bought	bought	grind	ground	ground
cast	cast	cast	grow	grew	grown
catch	caught	caught	hang	hung	hung[2]
choose	chose	chosen	have	had	had
cling	clung	clung	hear	heard	heard
come	came	come	hide	hid	hidden
cost	cost	cost	hit	hit	hit
creep	crept	crept	hold	held	held
cut	cut	cut	hurt	hurt	hurt
deal	dealt	dealt	keep	kept	kept
dig	dug	dug	know	knew	known
dive	dove/dived	dove/dived	lay	laid	laid
do	did	done	lead	led	led
draw	drew	drawn	leave	left	left

[2]*Hanged* is used as the past form to refer to punishment by death. *Hung* is used in other situations:
She *hung* the picture on the wall.

Base Form	Past Form	Past Participle	Base Form	Past Form	Past Participle
lend	lent	lent	split	split	split
let	let	let	spread	spread	spread
lie	lay	lain	spring	sprang	sprung
light	lit/lighted	lit/lighted	stand	stood	stood
lose	lost	lost	steal	stole	stolen
make	made	made	stick	stuck	stuck
mean	meant	meant	sting	stung	stung
meet	met	met	stink	stank	stunk
mistake	mistook	mistaken	strike	struck	struck/stricken
overcome	overcame	overcome	strive	strove	striven
overdo	overdid	overdone	swear	swore	sworn
overtake	overtook	overtaken	sweep	swept	swept
overthrow	overthrew	overthrown	swell	swelled	swelled/swollen
pay	paid	paid	swim	swam	swum
plead	pled/pleaded	pled/pleaded	swing	swung	swung
prove	proved	proven/proved	take	took	taken
put	put	put	teach	taught	taught
quit	quit	quit	tear	tore	torn
read	read	read	tell	told	told
ride	rode	ridden	think	thought	thought
ring	rang	rung	throw	threw	thrown
rise	rose	risen	understand	understood	understood
run	ran	run	uphold	upheld	upheld
say	said	said	upset	upset	upset
see	saw	seen	wake	woke	woken
seek	sought	sought	wear	wore	worn
sell	sold	sold	weave	wove	woven
send	sent	sent	wed	wedded/wed	wedded/wed
set	set	set	weep	wept	wept
sew	sewed	sewed/sewn	win	won	won
shake	shook	shaken	wind	wound	wound
shed	shed	shed	withhold	withheld	withheld
shine	shone/shined	shone/shined	withdraw	withdrew	withdrawn
shoot	shot	shot	withstand	withstood	withstood
show	showed	shown/showed	wring	wrung	wrung
shrink	shrank/shrunk	shrunk/shrunken	write	wrote	written
shut	shut	shut			
sing	sang	sung			
sink	sank	sunk			
sit	sat	sat			
sleep	slept	slept			
slide	slid	slid			
slit	slit	slit			
speak	spoke	spoken			
speed	sped	sped			
spend	spent	spent			
spin	spun	spun			
spit	spit/spat	spit/spat			

Note:

The past and past participle of some verbs can end in *-ed* or *-t.*

burn	burned or burnt
dream	dreamed or dreamt
kneel	kneeled or knelt
learn	learned or learnt
leap	leaped or leapt
spill	spilled or spilt
spoil	spoiled or spoilt

Map of the United States of America

AL	Alabama	HI	Hawaii	MA	Massachusetts	NM	New Mexico	SD	South Dakota
AK	Alaska	ID	Idaho	MI	Michigan	NY	New York	TN	Tennessee
AZ	Arizona	IL	Illinois	MN	Minnesota	NC	North Carolina	TX	Texas
AR	Arkansas	IN	Indiana	MS	Mississippi	ND	North Dakota	UT	Utah
CA	California	IA	Iowa	MO	Missouri	OH	Ohio	VT	Vermont
CO	Colorado	KS	Kansas	MT	Montana	OK	Oklahoma	VA	Virginia
CT	Connecticut	KY	Kentucky	NE	Nebraska	OR	Oregon	WA	Washington
DE	Delaware	LA	Louisiana	NV	Nevada	PA	Pennsylvania	WV	West Virginia
FL	Florida	ME	Maine	NH	New Hampshire	RI	Rhode Island	WI	Wisconsin
GA	Georgia	MD	Maryland	NJ	New Jersey	SC	South Carolina	WY	Wyoming
								DC*	District of Columbia

*The District of Columbia is not a state. Washington, D.C., is the capital of the United States.
Note: Washington, D.C., and Washington state are not the same.

Index

Photo Credits